Whiteness, Afrikaans, Afrikaners

Whiteness, Afrikaans, Afrikaners
Addressing Post-Apartheid Legacies, Privileges and Burdens

First published by the Mapungubwe Institute for Strategic Reflection (MISTRA) in 2018
142 Western Service Rd
Woodmead
Johannesburg, 2191

ISBN 978-0-6399238-1-9

© **MISTRA, 2018**
Production and design by Jacana Media, 2018
Editor in chief: Joel Netshitenzhe
Text editor: Barry Gilder
Copy editor: Christopher Merrett
Proofreader: Isabelle Delvare
Designer: Shawn Paikin
Set in Sabon 10.5/15pt
Printed and bound by Creda Communications
Job no. 003299

When citing this publication, please list the publisher as MISTRA.
All rights reserved. Without limiting the rights under copyright reserved above, no part of this publication may be reproduced, stored in or introduced into a retrieval system, or transmitted, in any form or by any means (electronic, mechanical, photocopying, recording or otherwise), without prior written permission of both the copyright holder and the publisher of the book.

This book is sold subject to the condition that it shall not, by way of trade or otherwise, be lent, re-sold, hired out or otherwise circulated without the publisher's prior consent in any form of binding or cover other than that in which it is published and without a similar condition being imposed on the subsequent purchaser.

Contents

Contributors vii
Preface xix
Acknowledgements xxi
Acronyms and Abbreviations xxiii

Keynote Address

Kgalema Motlanthe 1

Being White Today

Melissa Steyn – Whiteness: Post-apartheid, decolonial 9
Andries Nel – Where are the Suzmans, Slovos, Fischers
    and Naudés of today? 17
Mary Burton – The 'white man's burden': Fifteen years after
    the TRC 25
Christi van der Westhuizen – White power today 35

Whiteness and the South African Economy

Lynette Steenveld – Capitalism, racialism and whiteness 45

Bobby Godsell – The colour of capital...................................51
Dirk Hermann – Dear Mother Africa.....................................57
Ernst Roets – Double standards and black privilege: The new
             story of South Africa...65
Xhanti Payi – The demands of the new world sustain the
             sins of the old: The parks fable on transformation..73

The World of Ideas: The Place of Afrikaans
Mathatha Tsedu – The world of ideas: The place of Afrikaans.....87
Pieter Duvenage – Afrikaner intellectual history: An
                interpretation 91
Hein Willemse – The hidden histories of Afrikaans..................115
Nico Koopman – A South African ('n Suid Afrikaner)
              university: Is it possible?................................131

Closing Remarks
Achille Mbembe 141
Mathews Phosa..147

Contributors

Kgalema Motlanthe

Kgalema Petrus Motlanthe was born to a working-class family on 19 July 1949 in Alexandra Township, Johannesburg. He was elected President of the Republic of South Africa on 25 September 2008 and served until 9 May 2009.

After his retirement as President, Motlanthe was appointed by President Jacob Zuma to serve as the Deputy President and occupied that position from 11 May 2009 until 24 May 2014. As Deputy President, Motlanthe performed various functions, including the following:
- leader of government business in the National Assembly
- leader of the Anti-Poverty Programme
- chairperson of the Energy Advisory Council
- chairperson of the Human Resource Development Council
- chairperson of the South African National Aids Council
- chairperson of the Inter-Ministerial Committee for the 2010 FIFA World Cup.

In the 1970s, while working for the Johannesburg City Council, he was recruited into Umkhonto we Sizwe (MK), the then armed wing of the African National Congress (ANC). He was part of a unit tasked with recruiting members for military training outside the country.

On 14 April 1976 Motlanthe was arrested with others for furthering the aims of the ANC and kept in detention for eleven months at John Vorster Square in central Johannesburg. In 1977 he was found guilty on three charges under the Terrorism Act and sentenced to an effective ten years' imprisonment on Robben Island.

After his release in 1987, Motlanthe was tasked with strengthening the trade union movement in the country. To this end, he worked for the National Union of Mineworkers (NUM) as a national office bearer responsible for education. Among other things, he was involved in training workers to form shop steward committees.

In 1990, when the banning of the ANC and other political organisations was lifted, Motlanthe was tasked with re-establishing ANC structures in Gauteng Province. In 1992 he was elected General Secretary of the NUM, succeeding Cyril Ramaphosa who had been elected Secretary-General of the ANC.

Motlanthe also served two five-year terms as Secretary-General of the ANC, from December 1997 to December 2007. Motlanthe was Deputy President of the ANC from December 2007 to December 2012.

Melissa Steyn

Melissa Steyn holds the DST-NRF South African National Chair in Critical Diversity Studies and is the founding director of the Wits Centre for Diversity Studies. Her work engages with intersecting hegemonic social formations, but she is best known for her publications on whiteness and white identity in post-apartheid South Africa. Her book *Whiteness Just Isn't What It Used To Be: White Identity in a Changing South Africa* (2001) won the 2002 Outstanding Scholarship Award in International and Intercultural Communication from the National Communication Association in the United States. Her co-edited books include *The Prize and the Price: Shaping Sexualities in South Africa Volume 2* (2009), *Performing Queer: Shaping Sexualities in South Africa Volume 1* (2005), *Under Construction: Race and*

Identity in South Africa Today (2004) and *Cultural Synergy in South Africa: Weaving Strands of Africa and Europe* (1996).

Steyn was featured as one of Routledge's Sociology Super Authors for 2013.

Andries Nel

Andries Nel is South Africa's Deputy Minister for Co-operative Governance and Traditional Affairs. Elected to Parliament in 1994, he has been Deputy Minister for Justice and Constitutional Development, Deputy Chief Whip and has served on a wide range of portfolio and ad hoc committees. His constituency work has been in Pretoria Central, Centurion, Atteridgeville, Waterberg and Midvaal.

His activism began at high school in São Paulo, Brazil, where his parents were part of the diplomatic corps. As a student he participated in the National Union of South African Students and several other organisations. He co-ordinated the Lawyers for Human Rights Capital Punishment and Penal Reform Project between 1990 and 1994 and was a member of the national executive committee of the ANC Youth League from 1996 to 2001. He is currently the co-ordinator of legal monitoring on the ANC's National Elections Team. He holds a Bachelor of Civil Law from the University of Pretoria and is married to Kim Robinson, CEO of Renaissance Strategic Solutions.

Mary Burton

Mary Burton (full name: Maria Macdiarmid Ingouville Burton) was born in Buenos Aires, Argentina, and attended schools there and in São Paulo, Brazil. In 1961 she married Cape Town businessman Geoff Burton, and they have lived in South Africa since then. They have four sons and ten grandchildren.

In 1965 Burton joined the Black Sash, a women's organisation opposed to apartheid, and later various other civil and human rights organisations. She served as national president of the Black Sash from

1986 to 1990 and is currently a member of its Board of Trustees. In 1994 she served as Provincial Electoral Officer for the Western Cape in the country's first national democratic elections. In 1995 she was appointed by President Nelson Mandela as a commissioner with the Truth and Reconciliation Commission. She is a previous member of the Council of the University of Cape Town (UCT), and a past president of UCT's Convocation. She has a BA degree from UCT (1982), and in 2011 the university awarded her the degree of Doctor of Social Science, *honoris causa*. She is a member of the Board of Trustees of the Imam Abdullah Haron Education Trust. Awards: Order of Luthuli (Silver), 2003; Member of the Order of the Disa, 2004.

Christi van der Westhuizen

Christi van der Westhuizen (PhD) is associate professor in Sociology at the University of Pretoria. She is the author of *Sitting Pretty – White Afrikaans Women in Postapartheid South Africa* (2017), *White Power and the Rise and Fall of the National Party* (2007) and *Working Democracy: Perspectives on South Africa's Parliament at 20 Years* (2014). She has made contributions to books, including *In the Balance: South Africans Debate Reconciliation* (2010), and to various journals, including guest editorship of a special section in *African Studies* on Afrikaner identity (2012). Her working life started as a journalist at the independent anti-apartheid weekly *Vrye Weekblad* and she later worked as associate editor at the global news agency Inter Press Service. She received the Mondi Paper Newspaper Award for her political columns. She is a regular public commentator in the media and writes a monthly column for *Beeld/Netwerk24* and a Thought Leader blog. Van der Westhuizen held a postdoctoral fellowship with the Institute for Humanities in Africa, University of Cape Town, and a research associateship with the Institute for Reconciliation and Social Justice, University of the Free State. Her PhD is in Diversity Studies and her master's in Political Economy (*cum laude*).

Lynette Steenveld

Lynette Steenveld has lectured in the School of Journalism and Media Studies (SJMS) at Rhodes University since the mid-1980s. Her early academic focus was on film studies, in particular the politics of film in contributing to social change. Broadly, this led to the study of feminist film and African cinema, and, in particular, anti-apartheid documentary films produced by local filmmakers. Her interest in media and politics moved from film to print. In the early 2000s she was appointed as the Independent Newspapers Chair of Media Transformation at SJMS and worked with the newspaper industry to put in place various programmes to facilitate the diversification of the media industry. To this end she conducted workshops on racism in the media; xenophobia; and citizen journalism. Her main area of research has thus been on the media and the politics of identity, and, more recently, on print media sustainability.

She is also the chair of the Board of *Grocott's Mail*, the oldest independent newspaper in South Africa which is located in Makhanda.

Bobby Godsell

Bobby Godsell is the current chair of Business Leadership South Africa, an organisation representing some 80 of the largest businesses operating in South Africa. He serves on the boards of the Industrial Development Corporation and the London-listed Russian gold and silver mining company, Polymetal International. He serves as co-chair of the Millennium Labour Council, a social dialogue body involving business and labour leaders.

Godsell is married to Gillian, who is a research psychologist, and has three daughters.

Dirk Hermann

Dirk Hermann is currently the CEO of Solidarity. He also serves as chairman of Solidarity Helping Hand, Maroela Media and Kraal Publishers. He is frequently quoted in the South African media regarding labour-related and socio-political issues.

Hermann obtained a law degree, two honours degrees in Industrial Psychology and Industrial Sociology respectively, and master's and PhD degrees in Industrial Sociology, focusing on affirmative action, at North West University (NWU) (formerly Potchefstroom University for Christian Higher Education). He also completed a postgraduate diploma in labour law at the University of Johannesburg (formerly the Rand Afrikaans University). He currently sits on the NWU Board.

Hermann was born in 1972 and is married to Elsha. They have four daughters, Marisha, Minè, Elzaan and Hanri.

Ernst Roets

Ernst Roets was born in Pretoria on 5 September 1985. He grew up in Tzaneen in Limpopo Province. After matriculating at Merensky High School, he enrolled for an LLB at the University of Pretoria. During his studies, he served on various student societies and was also a member of the Student Representative Council and the Senate of the University of Pretoria. As a student activist, he was the founder and first national chairperson of AfriForum Youth.

In April 2011, Roets was promoted to the position of deputy CEO of AfriForum. He is a registered attorney, although he does not practise as such. His position at AfriForum includes managing the organisation's communications department, acting as spokesperson for the organisation and co-ordinating various campaigns. He is currently in the final stage of his master's degree in Public Law (LLM). His dissertation deals with the extent to which minority communities are protected by the South African Constitution. AfriForum is a civil rights organisation that deals with the protection of minority rights in South Africa.

Xhanti Payi

Xhanti Payi is an economist and the managing director at Nascence Advisory and Research, a strategy consulting and research outfit. He is also a columnist for *Business Day* and *Business Times*, and has contributed articles to international publications like the *Financial Times*.

As a public commentator, his views are regularly sought by local and international media, including eNCA and the BBC. Payi has worked as an analyst at Investec Wealth and Investment, an economist at Stanlib Asset Managers and a country risk manager at Standard Bank. With academic training from the University of Cape Town and the University of London, Payi is keenly interested in creating new knowledge to contribute to solutions to today's economic and business challenges. Payi also serves on the advisory panel to the Deputy Minister of Trade and Industry.

Mathatha Tsedu

Mathatha Tsedu is the executive director of the South African National Editors' Forum (SANEF), prior to which he was general manager for strategic development and projects at Media24 News. After serving as editor of *City Press*, he was head of the Media24 Journalism Academy, responsible for training working and learner journalists. He is a seasoned media trainer. He was, until September 2013, project director of the Print and Digital Media Transformation Task Team and before that he was project director of the Press Freedom Commission of South Africa, which was established in 2011 to look at the regulatory framework of print media in South Africa. He is a board member of the African Media Initiative. He has served as editor at a number of South African newspapers, namely *Sunday Times* and *City Press*; and as deputy head of news at the SABC. He was chairperson of the African Editors' Forum, which brings together editors and editorial executives from across the African continent.

He chaired SANEF for three consecutive years, and is also a member of council of the Council for the Advancement of the South African Constitution. Tsedu is a recipient of a number of awards, including the Nieman Fellowship at Harvard University, the Nat Nakasa Award for Courageous Journalism, the Mondi Shanduka Lifetime Achiever Award and the SANEF Wrottesley Award, the Media24 Newspapers All Time Legend Award and the Naspers Phil Weber Award. He served on the Task Group on Government Communications that devised the government's communications structure, leading to the creation of the Government Communication and Information System. Tsedu holds a BA Honours in Journalism and Media Studies from Wits University. He was banned for six years and detained several times by the apartheid government.

Pieter Duvenage

Pieter Duvenage (born 1963) has studied philosophy in South Africa (Stellenbosch, Pretoria and Port Elizabeth) and Germany (Göttingen and Frankfurt-am-Main). He received his doctorate in 1994 from the University of Port Elizabeth (now Nelson Mandela Metropolitan University).

Since his first position as senior lecturer (1995), he has lectured in philosophy from 1997 as an associate professor, full professor and visiting professor at various South African universities (Limpopo, Johannesburg and Nelson Mandela Metropolitan), and two Australian universities with campuses in South Africa (Bond and Monash). On 1 October 2011 he became full professor and head of the Department of Philosophy at the University of the Free State in Bloemfontein.

He is the author and co-author of four books and 40 accredited articles in journals and books. He specialises in political and social philosophy within the traditions of critical theory, phenomenology/hermeneutics and South African intellectual history. He has been a rated researcher under the National Research Foundation since 2003 (current rating C1), a member of the Akademie (Suid-Afrikaanse Akademie vir Wetenskap en Kuns) since 2002 and a past president of the Philosophical Society of Southern Africa (2005–2008). Since 2015 he has been a professorial fellow at the Centre for Collingwood Studies and British Idealism; honorary professor at the University of Cardiff; and editor of the *Journal for Contemporary History* (based at the University of the Free State in Bloemfontein).

Hein Willemse

Hein Willemse studied law and Afrikaans literature at the University of the Western Cape. He has earned the following qualifications: BA (Hons) (*cum laude*), MA (*cum laude*), MBL and D.Litt. He has published widely on Afrikaans language, literature and orature studies. He has also taught for extended periods in Mexico, the USA and Namibia. He recently served as president of the International Society for the Oral Literatures of Africa. He is a Professor of Literature in the Department of Afrikaans, University of Pretoria, and the current editor-in-chief of the multilingual African literary journal *Tydskrif vir Letterkunde* (www.letterkunde.up.ac.za).

Nico Koopman

Nico Koopman has been Acting Vice-Rector Social Impact, Transformation and Personnel at Stellenbosch University since 1 June 2015. He is dean of the Faculty of Theology, director of the Beyers Naudé Centre for Public Theology and Professor of Systematic Theology and Public Theology at Stellenbosch University. He is an ordained pastor of the Uniting Reformed Church in Southern Africa. Since 2008 he has been a member of the Council of the University of Stellenbosch. His research focuses on the meaning of faith for public life and he has published widely on themes in the field of public theology. He is chairperson of the Global Network for Public Theology. During the academic year of September 2007 to June 2008 he was public theologian-in-residence at the Center of Theological Inquiry in Princeton. As academic, public speaker and writer, he plays a leading role in public discourse in the academy, churches and broader society, both locally and internationally.

Achille Mbembe

Achille Mbembe, born in Cameroon, obtained his PhD in History at the Sorbonne in Paris in 1989 and a DEA in Political Science at the Institut d'Etudes Politiques (Paris). He was assistant professor of History at Columbia University, New York, from 1988 to 1991, a senior research fellow at the Brookings Institute in Washington, DC, from 1991 to 1992, associate professor of History at the University of Pennsylvania from 1992 to 1996, and executive director of the Council for the Development of Social Science Research in Africa in Dakar, Senegal, from 1996 to 2000. Achille was also a visiting professor at the University of California, Berkeley, in 2001, and a visiting professor at Yale University in 2003. He has written extensively on African history and politics, including *La Naissance du Maquis dans le Sud-Cameroun* (Paris: Karthala, 1996). *On the Postcolony* was published in Paris in 2000 in French and the English translation was published by the University of California Press, Berkeley in 2001. In 2015, Wits University Press published a new, African edition.

Mathews Phosa

Lawyer, ANC member, MK commander, member of the ANC negotiating team at the Convention for a Democratic South Africa (CODESA), former premier of Mpumalanga and previously treasurer-general of the ANC, Nakedi Mathews Phosa was born on 1 September 1952 in Mbombela Township, Nelspruit, Eastern Transvaal (now Mpumalanga). He grew up with his grandfather in a rural area near Potgietersrus (now Mokopane). He was educated at Maripi High School in Acornhoek and matriculated from Orhovelani High School in Thulamahashe. In 1981, he opened a legal practice in Nelspruit. He left the country in 1985, and in 1986 became the regional commander of MK, the military wing of the ANC, in Mozambique. Phosa was one of the ANC members instrumental in convincing King Sobhuza II of Swaziland not to accept the apartheid regime's offer to give him the kaNgwane and Ngwavuma districts. Phosa, as an MK leader, operated out of Mozambique in his native Eastern Transvaal in the 1980s. Following the unbanning of the ANC in 1990, he played an important role in transition initiatives, including CODESA. He had been one of the first four members of the ANC to enter South Africa from exile in 1990 to start the process of negotiation with the National Party (NP) when the ANC was unbanned. He was also head of the legal department of the ANC, in which capacity he often engaged in fierce debates with the Minister of Law and Order, Hernus Kriel, over issues such as the joint investigation by the South African Police and the ANC into the death of Chris Hani. At the ANC's 52nd National Conference, Phosa was elected treasurer-general. He was a member of the national executive committee of the ANC from 1999. After the first democratic elections in 1994, Phosa was appointed premier of Mpumalanga, a position he held until 1999. In 1995, the University of Boston awarded him an honorary doctorate.

Preface

In August 2015, the Mapungubwe Institute for Strategic Reflection (MISTRA) published the outcome of its research project on social cohesion entitled *Nation Formation and Social Cohesion: An Enquiry into the Hopes and Aspirations of South Africans*. In the preface to that publication, we asked the questions:

> *Besides geography, as well as economic and political systems, to what extent do South Africa's people constitute a nation? Do the erstwhile colonial settlers – who, unlike in most other parts of the postcolonial world, have decided in large numbers to make the country their permanent home – deserve equal recognition as members of the emergent nation?*

However, in retrospect we noted a gap in that publication – the absence of the voices of white South Africans. Therefore, as a further probing of this vexed topic (perhaps more vexed now as we reel under the recent blows of an apparent resurgence of crude public manifestations of racism and a hardening of attitudes on both sides of the racial divide), MISTRA, in partnership with the Friedrich Ebert Stiftung (FES) and the National Institute for the Humanities and Social Sciences (NIHSS), convened a round-table in November 2015 at the Women's Gaol on Constitution Hill with the title 'Whites,

Afrikaans, Afrikaners: Addressing Post-Apartheid Legacies, Privileges and Burdens'.

As was expected, the discourse at the round-table was rigorous. We are therefore pleased to publish in this volume the varied and provoking presentations at the event, including the keynote address by former President Kgalema Motlanthe and inputs from Melissa Steyn, Andries Nel, Mary Burton, Christi van der Westhuizen, Lynette Steenveld, Bobby Godsell, Dirk Hermann (of Solidarity), Ernst Roets (of AfriForum), Xhanti Payi, Mathatha Tsedu, Pieter Duvenage, Hein Willemse and Nico Koopman. Closing remarks were given by Achille Mbembe and Mathews Phosa.

These varied inputs probe a range of issues about whiteness in general and about the place of Afrikaners and the Afrikaans language in democratic South Africa. Perhaps the key lesson to come out of this discourse is that there is no homogeneity of views on these issues among white South Africans in general and Afrikaners in particular. In fact, at the round-table, and in these pages, one finds a multifaceted effort to scrub energetically at the boundaries that apartheid South Africa imposed on us all.

We express our profound appreciation to the authors and to all the participants at the round-table and to the FES and NIHSS for making this discourse possible. We have, as far as possible, tried to reproduce the timbre of the event itself.

Joel Netshitenzhe
Executive Director
MISTRA

Acknowledgements

MISTRA conveys its warm gratitude to the facilitators, speakers and participants at the round-table on which this publication is based, not just for their participation, but for the courage with which they tackled a fraught topic.

We, in particular, thank the Friedrich Ebert Stiftung (FES) and the National Institute for Humanities and Social Sciences (NIHSS) for partnering us in this project, and for their generous financial support to it.

We also extend thanks to Barry Gilder, who edited this publication; to the staff of MISTRA, who helped to make the event a great success; and to Jacana Media for the copy edit, design, layout and production of this book.

MISTRA funders

Though not directly involved with this project, MISTRA would nonetheless like to acknowledge its donors and funders for their support towards the Institute. They include:
- Absa
- Airports Company of South Africa (ACSA)
- Anglo Gold Ashanti

- Anglo Platinum
- Aspen Pharmacare
- Batho Batho Trust
- Brimstone
- Chancellor House
- Coca-Cola
- Development Bank of South Africa (DBSA)
- Discovery
- Encha Group Limited
- First Rand Foundation
- Goldman Sachs
- Industrial Development Corporation (IDC)
- Jackie Mphafudi
- Kumba Iron Ore
- Liliesleaf
- Lincoln Mali
- MTN
- Naspers
- National Advisory Council on Innovation (NACI)
- Oppenheimer Memorial Trust (OMT)
- People's Republic of China Embassy
- Robinson Ramaite
- Safika
- Simeka Group
- South African Breweries (SAB)
- Standard Bank
- Thandi Ndlovu
- Transnet Foundation
- True Spark Investment
- UBU Holdings
- University of Johannesburg
- University of Pretoria
- University of the Witwatersrand
- Yellowwoods

Acronyms and Abbreviations

ANC	African National Congress
BEE	black economic empowerment
CEO	chief executive officer
CODESA	Convention for a Democratic South Africa
COSATU	Congress of South African Trade Unions
DST-NRF	Department of Science and Technology-National Research Foundation
FES	Friedrich Ebert Stiftung
FOSATU	Federation of South African Trade Unions
GDP	gross domestic product
GRA	Genootskap van Regte Afrikaanders
HRC	Human Rights Commission
JSE	Johannesburg Stock Exchange
MISTRA	Mapungubwe Institute for Strategic Reflection
MK	Umkhonto we Sizwe
NDP	National Development Plan
NIHSS	National Institute for the Humanities and Social Sciences
NP	National Party
NUM	National Union of Mineworkers
NWU	North West University
RDP	Reconstruction and Development Programme

SACP	South African Communist Party
SANEF	South African National Editors Forum
TRC	Truth and Reconciliation Commission
UCT	University of Cape Town
UWC	University of the Western Cape
VOC	Dutch East India Company
ZAR	South African Republic

Keynote Address

KGALEMA MOTLANTHE

Programme Director, Ms Gail Smith;
Deputy Minister, Mr Andries Nel;
MISTRA's Executive Director, Mr Joel Netshitenzhe;
MISTRA's Director of Operations, Mr Barry Gilder;
His Excellency, Ambassador Yacoob Abba Omar;
Delegates and participants;
Friends and comrades;
Distinguished guests;
Ladies and gentlemen:

I am pleased to join you today as we undertake to discourse on a topic we rarely converse about in South Africa; namely, whiteness and what it means, or should mean, in post-apartheid society.

I would therefore like to take this opportunity to thank the organisers of this round-table, the Mapungubwe Institute (MISTRA).

In this regard, you have dared to provide a platform for all of us to understand the history of whiteness in all its socio-economic manifestations as well as the architecture of its power relations and privileges.

At issue here is the imperative to interrogate a socially pernicious ideology intellectually identified as whiteness, which has historically privileged a particular racially defined social group by dint of skin colour.

The importance of this area of knowledge becomes all too apparent in the light of recent events on our social landscape, from the student protests against fee increases, growing calls for transformation of both our public and private institutions, and the call for decolonisation of the curriculum and staff representivity.

Weaving all these events together is the perception, rightly or wrongly, depending on one's social and ideological position, that identity issues are still unresolved two decades into our system of constitutional democracy.

We would do well to remember that the preamble to our Constitution enjoins us to prioritise the creation of 'a society based on democratic values, social justice and fundamental human rights'.

We are inclined to ask, therefore, what hampers the full realisation of these human rights and freedoms? Indeed, racial discrimination is neither permissible in our legislative framework nor allowed in the public domain. Yet this has not prevented the perception that the white section of our society is able to grow as a group thanks to racially favourable conditions, at least at a nuanced level.

In explaining this phenomenon, the one theory blames wilful ignorance, from an intellectual viewpoint, in terms of social practices rooted in notions of whiteness.

We either avoid an open, dispassionate public reflection on the scourge of racism or simply downplay it through all manner of subterfuge.

This is an astonishing act by intellectuals of all descriptions who avert their eyes to this historical sore point, given that South Africa is a colonial construct, meaning the notion of racism, or racialism, is rooted in its historical framework.

The one anomaly resulting from this wilful ignorance is that, while we hype up issues of racism in daily life, we scarcely ever dwell on its underlying causes.

To that extent this platform, which seeks to reflect on whiteness as a social construct, assumes epic proportions. As such one can only hope that this engagement will serve as an entry point for the emergence of a multiplicity of voices reflecting the full spectrum of our nation and seeking to confront the historical import of the ideology of whiteness from different angles.

To reiterate: my understanding of its stated objectives is that this round-table discussion is an attempt to untangle the webs of mystification surrounding the foundations of whiteness.

In this respect, let me make so bold as to offer a few thoughts on these underlying causes.

First, one may contend that whiteness is a global phenomenon that traces its privileged position to the eighteenth-century industrial revolution from which has evolved modernity.

More than any other epoch in history, the dawn of industrialism disproportionately empowered Europeans in comparison to the rest of the world.

The advent of the Middle Passage, or the transatlantic slave trade, during which black Africans were turned into chattels in the service of emerging capitalist needs from the sixteenth through to the nineteenth century, provided for and was based on notions not only of racial purity but supremacy.

Corresponding with the ascendant narrative of whiteness against the background of European modernisation, history was revised and many non-Western cultures were consciously debased and devalued.

In consequence, the central ontological narrative of human history was Europeanised.

And, therefore, to advance a more inclusive narrative, all conscious efforts have to be made to decentre whiteness through the creation of spaces for marginalised narratives, all of which have an equally justifiable claim to the centre of historical consciousness.

Second, related to the centredness of whiteness is the reality that it has over time commandeered the position of the normal and normative. Non-Europeans have not only been othered but also defined in reference to the white as a norm.

Richard Dyer, in his classic 1997 book, *White*, is apposite when he says: 'As long as race is something only applied to non-white people, as long as white people are not racially seen and named, they function as a human norm. Other people are raced, we are not. The claim to power is the claim to speak for the commonality of humanity. Raced people can't do that – they can only speak for their race'.

Third, the question that arises in dislodging whiteness from its perch of normativity is what it should be replaced by. The narratives of others should be elevated to the same position of privilege as the dominant Western canons with which modern history is familiar.

A closer look into human history shows that the pool of human knowledge has incrementally benefited from all humanity across the ages, with each ethnic or racial group having had its turn at one historical period or another.

Ancient China, India and Africa have each made notable contributions to the march of progress since antiquity, a fact that is not faithfully reflected in school curricula.

Instead, the Western canon of the so-called dead white men like Plato, Newton, Kant, Marx and Wittgenstein rule the roost, while non-Western figures such as al-Khwarizmi, who mathematised science, and the Chinese polymath scholar, Shen Kuo, as well as the African, Imhotep, the first recorded genius of antiquity, and many more, languish at the margins of history.

This is the reason I wish to commend the vice-chancellor of the University of Johannesburg, Dr Ihron Rensburg, who has undertaken to 'establish inclusive traditions, with particular reference to Africa'.

I believe this effort will incorporate Key Themes in African History, Great African Philosophers of the Nineteenth and Twentieth Centuries, Important Anti-Colonial Struggles of the 20th Century, The State of the Post-colony – Progress and Retrogression, and Critical Citizenship in the 21st Century.

Fourth, these initiatives – partly aimed at removing whiteness from its unfairly privileged historical standing – also call for recognition that whiteness comes with access to power invariably expressed through the economic apparatus that enables it to include and exclude.

This power mechanism wielded by the ideology of whiteness was emphasised recently by the pronouncements of a prominent white human rights lawyer who tried to defend his decision for only briefing and working with white lawyers, since, in his opinion, only they have the cognitive capabilities to close and win cases.

Fifth, acknowledging whiteness as a social and historical construct like blackness, is an urgent reminder to all progressive forces to keep up the intellectual fight to reconstruct our world in line with non-racial principles.

The one area where more work can be directed to build a non-racial society is education. In this regard, I was given to understand that Professor Melissa Steyn of Wits University has provided a sterling example through her decades-long project of focusing on critical whiteness studies.

Her course, Critical Diversity Literacy, constitutes an intellectual matrix not only for helping to challenge the reigning toxic culture of 'whiteness' and other forms of social domination but also by offering alternative world views that embrace our common humanity.

My understanding of the thrust of her project is that it seeks to communicate the point that there are certain hegemonic identities that are taken as given – like whiteness – which must now be supplemented by other forms of literacy which, as we have argued, constitute other social markers that have been marginalised in our past.

Furthermore, we would do well to realise that the presence of these social identities is felt in our daily lives, including female oppression, religious discrimination, discrimination based on sexuality, and so on.

On a broader level, we need to understand that there is more than one form of discrimination and that, in order to build a new world, our efforts have to be directed at all forms.

All these baleful thoughts and acts stain our human rights experience and disfigure the ultimate goal of deepening democracy and freedom for all sectors of society.

Programme Director:

By way of conclusion, let me remind us that our globalised world has rendered social, political and economic identities both fragmented and homogenised.

This paradoxical process offers opportunities to rethink our identities by focusing on our primary identity as human beings who share one common future.

Whether we are black or white, the modern challenges staring us in the face are the same. We face an uncertain future resulting from global warming, social inequality, unemployment, poverty, violence and corruption.

Racial divisions drawing sustenance from economically defined racial consciousness may serve us well in our narrow enclaves, but will not help us grapple with the imperatives of the age.

The act of debunking whiteness has to be seen as a shared moral duty for all of us who believe in the possibility of a non-racial future.

In the long run, building an inclusive society grounded in high-minded consciousness of a shared humanity is a possibility worth pursuing.

In this regard we should be guided by the preamble of our Constitution, which stipulates that: 'This Constitution is the supreme law of the Republic' and 'All citizens are equally entitled to the rights, privileges and benefits of citizenship: and equally subject to the duties and responsibilities of citizenship.'

I thank you.

Being White Today

Whiteness

Post-apartheid, decolonial

MELISSA STEYN

Whiteness, post-apartheid

The political changes of 1994 altered the power relations between differently racialised groups in South Africa irrevocably, from the violent subjugation of the majority by a white minority in every dimension of national life, to a constitutional democracy. An era of renegotiating identities and of working through the terms of national belonging was ushered in.

According to Terreblanche (2002), the negotiated settlement secured the economic position of white South Africans. This meant that there was no simple reversal in power relations, despite the end of white supremacist rule. With the national project articulated in terms of reconciliation rather than liberation (Mpofu and Sonderling, in press), black South Africans were asked to forgive white South Africans for the injustices of the past; while white South Africans, in effect, were invited to be more inclusive and sharing in the organisation of the national economy, a bidding mandated through legislation introducing affirmative action, employment equity and black economic empowerment. While the Truth and Reconciliation Commission (TRC) exacted some acknowledgement of the depth and extent of the suffering endured by black South Africans, no apology, no symbolic or material gesture of reparation, was asked of white South Africans; nor were any offered.

White South Africans experienced the transition to democracy as ushering in vulnerability, not only because majority rule transferred the levers of state power that had sustained minority rule throughout the history of whiteness in South Africa, but also because they were now more exposed to scrutiny from those whose voices and observations were previously suppressed. This required, even if only implicitly, giving an account of themselves and their past participation in apartheid, reframed in relation to a present and future that had to be based on a different relationship to black South Africa (Steyn, 2001). This tacit onus has applied especially to Afrikaners, who were most overtly implicated in institutionalising and supporting apartheid, and who could not deny their culpability, unlike English South Africans who, despite being beneficiaries of the 'racial contract' (Mills, 1999), were able to claim not to have been signatories to it during the apartheid period. Much of the operation of whiteness in post-apartheid South Africa has in fact been a scramble to avoid actually stepping up to this accountability.

By and large, white South Africans have dealt with their changed political circumstances by thoroughly deploying the cultural capital of whiteness to influence, and even where possible control, the dominant understandings of critical issues within South Africa so as to stem the erosion of the privilege that their whiteness affords them. This has included appropriating aspects of the dominant party's language where possible. Under the hegemonic operations of 'white talk', non-racialism – which historically advocated a form of race-cognisant inclusivity, mutated into colour blindness – and neo-liberal economic policies have been advanced as the only viable road for the country's development.

Three ways in which white South Africans have created distance between themselves and accountability for the past are through constructing innocence, withdrawing, and claiming victim status. To construct innocence, a remarkable amount of discursive creativity has been displayed to claim that white people were ignorant of what happened under apartheid. This in turn obviates the need for serious self-reflection and means that whites claiming such innocence do not feel an obligation to negotiate a real relationship with their compatriots. Withdrawal has been achieved through retreating into private spaces, such as 'semigration' to elite neighbourhoods (Ballard, 2004), the private sector, private schools and private discursive spaces. The final mechanism has been the construction of themselves as victims: first of affirmative action, even in the face of statistics that indicate that the employment bias remains stacked against black South Africans; and second of a general decline in standards and lowered expectations, which they have to circumvent through private means of organisation; and even accusations of genocide, as in the right-wing rhetoric of farm murders. This victimhood legitimises nostalgia for a lost world in which things were apparently/allegedly still functional. All of these show a commitment to ignorance about how black South Africans have been, and continue to be, affected by the pervasive white preference of the system. All of them reposition white South Africans outside the project of national reconciliation. It is, quite simply, not their problem.

Whiteness, the decolonial turn?

The advent of democracy in South Africa occurred at a time when the theorisation of race and racism within academia was also undergoing a sea change. The implications of social construction and discourse theory were being recognised in a shift away from understanding race as biologically determined groupings to social groups formed within unequal power relations, the biological differences merely being convenient markers on which systems of domination and subordination, privilege and oppression have been pegged. This in turn largely shifted the analytical gaze from the personal, psychological attributes of individuals, such as prejudice, to racialised subjectivities shaped within a social positionality of relative advantage – whiteness – and those constructed within relational disadvantage – blackness – through the same social and economic dynamics.

Within the more recent past, new discourses have emerged that may be ushering in a new phase for whiteness in South Africa. The lens of decoloniality, brought to the fore by the student movement of 2015, extends both the depth and scope of the analysis of race and racialisation in our context. For one, while much of the popular and social analytic discourse has generally focused on the apartheid era, decolonial theory emphasises the longer arc of coloniality (Maldonados-Torres, 2007). We have therefore seen that the #RhodesMustFall student movement did not reproduce the tendency to render invisible that part of South African history that implicates the Anglo actors; but identifies earlier colonial atrocities and sees the injuries to blackness in the post-1910 union as part of a continuum with apartheid. This means that no white South Africans can construct themselves as exempt from giving account.

The emerging consciousness is well versed in the insights wrought by studies of whiteness and blackness, and indeed, intersectionality; these are the discourses shaping so-called fallist subjectivities and are being drawn on to make sense of people's realities. They refer to black pain, the suffering wrought by experiencing indignity and ongoing undervaluation, the trivialisation of black experience, and the struggle for opportunity. The self-interested mechanisms of white privilege are not obscure to many of this generation. There is a marked shift to analyses that foreground how racial injustice has been the organising logic of our social formation over generations, rather than merely residing in the acts of a few nasty individuals. This allows for a much more trenchant understanding of how the ideologies of coloniality have created a world that is systematically and consistently inclined in favour of those of European stock and is stacked against those who are black, especially through the operations of whiteness as the norm. Once the normative order is in place, it reproduces itself – dominated by, centred on, and identified with, whiteness (Johnson, 2001). The views of those who are privileged by being in this normative space are taken more seriously. They are seen as more authoritative, more competent, and what happens to them is regarded as more newsworthy – these dynamics work through all levels of social organisation. Such expectations still pervade white South African spaces – expectations of being the norm, and that society should reproduce itself for their psychological, material, cultural and economic comfort. Systemic, and indeed systematic, societal preference is simply seen as the recognition of their capabilities and worth.

The question that arises is how white South Africans will deal with this new wave of awareness and self-assertion in black South Africans. It seems that many have not done the necessary homework for the first phase of racial realignment that played itself out in the first twenty years of democracy, a phase which in truth required little more than recognition of the damage, injury and hurt wrought by the unjust past, and a willingness to be less exclusionary. More often, these have been construed as unreasonable impositions. Because this homework has not been done, many will be unprepared for the new phase in which the hegemony of whiteness will surely unravel even more.

The challenge is whether, in a context where whiteness does not dominate the organs of the state, and is profoundly challenged in other social domains, it can reconfigure itself as supportive, not dominant, as it has operated historically. For this, white South Africans will have to do the difficult work of recognising the relational nature of racial formations, acknowledge the implication of whiteness in racial injustice, and display a willingness to work for a different social compact. In all likelihood, the next years will demand much more identification with African priorities and recognition of the need for systematic black advancement.

Decolonising whiteness will require much more than just rehearsing the widely acknowledged implications of white privilege, and its concomitant blindness and ignorance. A decolonised whiteness would mean changes in all facets of being – cognitive and epistemological, affective and ethical. A starting point would be for white people to educate themselves about the realities of black lives, and not only those that reflect back to them a sense of comfort with their whiteness, such as the black middle classes and the so-called elite blacks, who are doing well, often assimilate white norms, and are relatively unchallenging to their consciences. White South Africa will need to exert itself to understand what people mean when they write about black pain, the realities of the majority of black lives, which still carry the burden of colonial and apartheid economic and social violence and continue to be positioned within poverty, hardship and lives of indignity – those lives which challenge white people to look into the harsh truths of what white supremacy has constructed in their names. This will mean taking a serious, unflinching relook at history, understanding how whiteness contributed to the colonial project, and how whites were educated to be comfortable with unjust political and economic orders. It will mean educating their emotions, as indifference is not an ethical response in such an asymmetrical arrangement. It will require moving from denial and avoidance of uncomfortable emotions, through the temptation to escape into white fragility or retreat into spaces where secret lives of hostility to the demands of the current society can be lived. Rather, they should feel emotions appropriate to the decolonial context – which may include some guilt and shame, but also outrage at inequality and suffering, compassion and generosity as they recognise the need for a radical rearrangement of society. It is a stance that takes responsibility and remains engaged and committed to the project of building a society on different principles. Such a changed alignment of racial power revises citizenship into mutual relationship, mutual responsibility.

Only time will tell if whiteness will, or even can, decolonise.

References

Ballard, R. (2004) 'Assimilation, emigration, semigration, and integration: "white" peoples' strategies for finding a comfort zone in post-apartheid South Africa'. In Distiller, N. and Steyn, M. (eds). *Under Construction: 'Race' and Identity in South Africa Today*. Cape Town: Heinemann.

Johnson, A.G. (2001) *Privilege, Power and Difference*. Mountain View, CA: Mayfield Publishing Company.

Maldonado-Torres, N. (2007) 'On the coloniality of being'. *Cultural Studies* 21(2–3): 240–270.

Mills, C. W. (1997) *The Racial Contract*. Ithaca, NY: Cornell University Press.

Mpofu, W. and Sonderling, S. (in press) 'Coloniality at large: the South African TRC as the manufacture of political consent'. *Communication*.

Steyn, M.E. (2001) *Whiteness Just Isn't What It Used To Be: White Identity in a Changing South Africa*. Albany, NY: State University of New York Press.

Terreblanche, S.J. (2002) *A History of Inequality in South Africa 1652–2002*. Pietermaritzburg: University of KwaZulu-Natal Press.

Where are the Suzmans, Slovos, Fischers and Naudés of today?

ANDRIES NEL

Ben Okri writes in *A Way of Being Free* that 'The worst realities of our age are manufactured realities. It is our task, as creative participants in the universe, to redream our world. The fact of possessing imagination means that everything can be redreamed. Each reality can have its alternative possibilities. Human beings are blessed with the necessity of transformation.'

I have been asked to answer the question: 'Where are the Suzmans, Slovos, Fischers and Naudés of today?' Often, asking the right question is as, if not more, important than getting the right answer.

Helen Suzman, Joe Slovo, Bram Fischer and Beyers Naudé no doubt were all, albeit in very different ways, 'creative participants in the universe' and were 'blessed with the necessity of transformation.'

But is this the right question to be asking? What, in fact, is being asked?

Suzman, Slovo, Fischer and Naudé are an interesting choice on which to frame the question.

Fischer was born in 1908, Naudé in 1915, Suzman in 1917 and

Slovo in 1926. They experienced colonialism of a special type in the context of the global rise and consolidation of the nation state.

All were white. One was a woman. Suzman and Slovo were born into Jewish families, Fischer and Naudé into Christian families. Suzman attended a convent school.

Suzman and Slovo were born of Lithuanian immigrants. Today they would be called refugees.

Suzman and Slovo were English-speaking, Fischer and Naudé Afrikaans-speaking.

Fischer's father was Judge-President of the Orange Free State, his grandfather Prime Minister of the Orange River Colony. Naudé's father was a dominee and a founder member of the Afrikaner Broederbond. Slovo left school at fifteen to work and studied law after World War II on an ex-serviceman's scholarship. #FeesFellForSlovo.

All of them benefitted, in different ways, from the system they opposed.

Suzman was a liberal who believed in parliamentary opposition; Naudé a radical Christian who was banned. Fischer and Slovo were leaders of the Communist Party and the ANC, who engaged in armed struggle against apartheid. They were arrested, imprisoned or exiled.

They were all leaders, in different ways. But this begs the questions: Were they leaders of the white community? Were they leaders in the white community? Were they white individuals whose beliefs led them to oppose injustice, albeit in very different ways?

Their lives demonstrate that all people have multiple identities. This reality is accentuated in South Africa by history and circumstance.

They demonstrate that leaders are shaped by their societies much as their societies are also shaped by individual and collective action.

The question: Where are the Suzmans, Slovos, Fischers and Naudés of today? can, I believe, only be addressed in relation to the circumstances and the challenges of today.

Central to these challenges are poverty, inequality and unemployment, and the racial form that they take.

Almost 45 years ago, Rick Turner argued in *The Eye of the Needle* that:

Where are the Suzmans, Slovos, Fischers and Naudés of today?

South Africa, everyone agrees, is a profoundly unequal society. It is marked by inequality of power, of wealth, of access to the means for acquiring power and/or wealth, of education, and of status.

This much is agreed upon. Disagreement arises, however, when the causes of this situation are sought. Most whites see these inequalities as being the result of the unequal contribution made by the various ethnic groups. The whites have 'brought civilization', developed industry, etc., and it is only natural that they should take the lion's share. The blacks have not really contributed, either because they are biologically inferior, or because they are culturally inferior. There is disagreement as to whether and when this cultural gap can be bridged, but there is wide agreement that it existed in the first place and is at the origin of today's inequalities. Most blacks, on the other hand, see these inequalities as being largely the result of exploitation and of inequality of opportunity.

In South Africa the major cause of conflict is the unequal distribution of wealth. This unequal distribution coincides almost exactly with color or race differences, and somewhat more roughly, with cultural differences.

Neither cultural nor racial differences are in themselves inherently causes of social conflict, although they can, through ignorance and prejudice, become causes of conflict.

In South Africa, this basic cause of social conflict and tension is overlaid by race and cultural prejudice in a potent mixture. Prejudice can be cured by education. Contradiction of interest cannot.

However, if the wealth gap is done away with, there will no longer be any inherent reason for conflict. Cultural or racial groups can and do co-exist when they are not also divided by different economic interests.

The maintenance of their cultural identity by white South Africans is a reasonable wish, but it is not dependent on their maintenance of economic privilege, and should not be confused with this.

> *The whites are, in an important sense, themselves victims of the very system that they fight to preserve. For in becoming racialists and exploiters they become closed off to important areas of human experience.*
>
> *We have already discussed in general terms what is meant by the injunction 'love your neighbour as yourself.' To be yourself, you must love your neighbour. The question is, what do you become if you fear and hate your neighbour?*
>
> *The essential thing that white South Africans lose is openness to the future and to other people.*
>
> *We must attack racism, but we must also attack the unquestioned acceptance of material values underlying racism. We must try to show to all those who accept the dominant values how much they lose in this society and how much they could gain in a good society. 'Self-interest' and 'material interest' are not the same. In fact, they are often incompatible.*

The struggle to which the Suzmans, Slovos, Fischers and Naudés contributed has created the conditions to realise, in Ben Okri's words, 'alternative possibilities'.

The latest incarnation of our attempt to 'redream' our society in line with the 'necessity of transformation' spelled out in our Constitution is encapsulated in the National Development Plan (NDP).

The NDP envisions a South Africa where everyone feels free yet bonded to others; where everyone embraces their full potential; a country where opportunity is determined not by birth, but by ability, education and hard work.

Realising such a society will require transformation of the economy in ways that benefit all South Africans as well as focused efforts to build the country's capabilities.

Young people deserve better educational and economic opportunities, and focused efforts are required to eliminate gender inequality. Levels of frustration and impatience are rising. Time is of the essence.

Achieving social cohesion is central to the NDP. It makes the point strongly that, if we deracialise ownership and control of the economy without reducing poverty and inequality, transformation will be superficial. Conversely, if poverty and inequality are reduced without demonstrably changed ownership patterns, the country's progress will be turbulent and tenuous.

Progress over the next two decades will mean doing things differently. The NDP sets out six interlinked priorities:

> *First, uniting all South Africans around a common programme to achieve prosperity and equity;*
> *Second, promoting active citizenry to strengthen development, democracy and accountability;*
> *Third, bringing about faster economic growth, higher investment and greater labour absorption;*
> *Fourth, focusing on key capabilities of people and the State;*
> *Fifth, building a capable and developmental State;*
> *Sixth, encouraging strong leadership throughout society to work together to solve problems.*

The successful implementation of the NDP requires strong leadership from, and within, government, business, labour and civil society.

Leaders throughout society are required to work together, to break with the tendency to advocate positions that promote narrow, short-term interests at the expense of a broader, long-term agenda.

I would argue that this is where the Suzmans, Slovos, Fischers and Naudés of today must be found and be encouraged to emerge: to make a contribution as citizens, citizens with the benefit of accumulated advantages, but not as messiahs.

We need partnerships across society working together towards a common purpose. We need to overcome the high levels of mistrust between major social partners.

Leaders in government must shoulder a large share of responsibility for implementing the NDP, while working with others in society to do so.

This means being prepared to take difficult decisions and trade-offs and persuade society of the correctness of these decisions. This requires communicating honestly and sincerely. It also requires the moral authority and legitimacy to do so.

The state sets an example for society. If corruption is seen as acceptable in government, it will affect the way society conducts itself and undermine the moral authority of the state. This makes combating corruption a priority for all leaders.

Successful implementation of the NDP will also require leadership in the private sector. The private sector must invest in productive capacity. We need leaders who understand that, while the profit motive drives business, companies cannot grow unless employment and income levels are rising.

The long-term interests of all businesses require the country to grow faster and have more people employed. It is also in the interests of business that the level of inequality be reduced. Inequality fuels mistrust and tension. It also raises the cost of doing business, skews market structure and ultimately limits growth opportunities. Obscenely generous executive remuneration does little to foster a sense of inclusivity and shared benefit in the fruits of development.

Union leadership is also crucial. Historically, trade union leaders have understood that issues affecting their members do not stop at the factory gate and have played a role in politics.

Gains by union members must be sustainable in the long term. To achieve this, productivity and employment have to rise continuously. Outcomes determined in bargaining processes must not close the door for new entrants to the workplace.

Leadership is required to ensure that unions share responsibility for the quality of services delivered, for improving the performance of government, and for fighting corruption and inefficiency.

Leadership in civil society forms an integral part of a vibrant democracy that involves people in their own development. Leaders are responsible for ensuring that criticism and protest are conducted with dignity and maturity.

In the past few months we have seen, through the student movement, the emergence of a 'generation' in the sense in which the term has been used historically in the liberation movement. We must encourage this trend and engage in an inter-generational dialogue.

References

National Development Plan 2030: Our Future: Make it Work. (2011) National Planning Commission.

Okri, B. (1997) *A Way of Being Free.* London: Phoenix.

Turner, R. (1972) *The Eye of the Needle: Towards Participatory Democracy in South Africa.* Johannesburg: Christian Institute of Southern Africa.

The 'white man's burden'
Fifteen years after the TRC

MARY BURTON

The years that have passed since the promulgation of the Promotion of National Unity and Reconciliation Act in 1995, and the completion of the work of the TRC by 2002, provide an opportunity to consider what degree of unity and reconciliation has been achieved between the people of South Africa since then.

The recommendations of the TRC are contained in its report delivered to President Nelson Mandela in October 1998. In some 50 pages in volume five, they cover a range of topics, including justice, health, the private sector, the media, education, traditional affairs, the security forces, healing and rehabilitation, the faith communities, as well as reparations and restitution for suffering as a result of 'gross violations of human rights'.

These recommendations are preceded by an introduction urging all South Africans to work towards national reconciliation and unity, and arguing that a prerequisite for this would be the furthering of a strong human rights culture and the closing of 'the intolerable gap between the advantaged and the disadvantaged in our society'. The commission recommended that a scheme be put into place to enable those who benefited from apartheid policies to contribute towards the alleviation of poverty (TRC *Report*, v.5: 308).

Two matters that arose during the drafting of the recommendations were lustration (disqualification of persons from certain categories of public office if they had been found responsible for gross violations of human rights) and a wealth tax. The commission decided not to recommend lustration, nor, in its first report, to recommend a wealth tax, although it listed this as one of several mechanisms that should be considered (including a one-off levy on corporate and private income, a retrospective surcharge on corporate profits, and a surcharge on golden handshakes given to public servants since 1990) (TRC *Report*, v.5: 318, 319). However, a further list of recommendations was introduced in its final report that did include a 'once-off wealth tax on South African business and industry' (TRC *Report*, v.6: 727).

Furthermore, it recommended a Business Reconciliation Fund designed to implement development options such as grants or loans for black small entrepreneurs, in addition to the provision of skills training and affirmative action programmes.

The TRC requested the President of South Africa 'to call a National Summit on Reconciliation, not only to consider the specific recommendations ... but to ensure maximum involvement ... in the pursuit of reconciliation ... [This] Summit should be held towards the end of 1999' [TRC] *Report*, v.5: 304–305).

As events turned out, the presentation on 29 October 1998 of the Interim Report, as the first five volumes were described, was almost prevented by court actions against the commission, first by ex-President F.W. de Klerk, and then, at the last moment, by the ANC. The former was settled by agreement, and the latter by the court's ruling in favour of the TRC. Although this enabled the presentation and dissemination of the report to proceed, it inevitably led to a cooling of the relationship between the commission and the ANC. When the report was formally presented to a joint sitting of Parliament on 25 February 1999, it was very clear that findings made against the ANC remained a bitter source of resentment for many of its representatives.

After October 1998, the major portion of the commission's work had been completed, but its Amnesty Committee was authorised to continue until a final dissolution date, set for 31 March 2002. It would also have responsibility for any uncompleted matters arising from the functions of the other two committees – the Reparations and Rehabilitation Committee; and the Committee for Gross Violations of Human Rights. The final two volumes of the report were eventually completed in 2002, presented to President Thabo Mbeki, and discussed in Parliament in early 2003.

It remains a source of profound disappointment to many, inside and outside the TRC itself, that the long period which elapsed between the 1998 report and the final discussion of its recommendations by Parliament, left the approximately 22,000 victims of violations in a state of anxious anticipation. During that time, many of them were in situations of desperate need, and had come to expect that some of that need would be met by the reparations recommended. When the government announced that these would be considerably less than had been proposed, there was widespread disappointment and anger. At the same time, thousands more people claimed they had been left out of the process and have continued to express their frustration.

During those four intervening years, a number of analyses of the TRC's work were published and debated, many with a focus on whether and how reconciliation and redress might be part of the outcome of its work. Ugandan scholar Mahmoud Mamdani was at the forefront of those who blamed the commission for neglecting the role of the beneficiaries of apartheid. The mandate to address the actions of perpetrators was seen as having exonerated those white South Africans who might not have committed any individual actions of violation of human rights, yet who had remained silent while receiving all the privileges of their status, and/or continued to vote for the policies of discrimination.

In recent years there has been further attention paid to whiteness (or whiteliness) in pursuit of the goal of reducing the uneven relations of power and wealth that continue to divide the population. Such attention has sometimes been critical of what is seen as an inward-looking examination, especially when it allows for an identity of victimhood for white people, or for their denial of responsibility for the past and for on-going benefits resulting from the policies of apartheid.

By no means did all such beneficiaries feel exonerated. During the life of the TRC, the commissioners heard many messages from white South Africans, within the country and abroad, expressing gratitude for the opportunity to reflect on the past, and conveying their regret for ways in which they believed they had contributed to injustice either by commission or by neglecting to act. Some of them expressed the wish to make up in some way for this. In response, the TRC set up a Reconciliation Register, where such feelings could be recorded. It clearly met a need, as letters and messages flowed in, and sometimes individuals or groups came into the offices to sign the register and to write some expression of their experience.

In 2000, after the conclusion of the first part of the TRC's existence, a group based in Cape Town established the Home for All campaign, taking for its inspiration the words of Chief Albert Luthuli: 'The task is not yet finished. South Africa is not yet a home for all its sons and daughters'. Its goal was to offer an opportunity for white people to acknowledge that they had received, and continued to receive, benefits from apartheid policies, even if they had been actively opposed to them. In response, they were invited to commit themselves to making a contribution towards the success of the new government's commitments to reconstruction and development, by making donations or assisting the process of reconciliation in any way they could. The campaign did not require an apology, nor was it an attempt to impose guilt, but from the start it was rejected by many who interpreted it that way. It was a step too far for most white people to take (Mathews, 2010).

It is a dozen years since then, and it would be difficult to imagine even embarking on such a project today. Many white citizens, possibly reacting to policies of affirmative action in the spheres of employment and education, or to resentment at being asked to accept responsibility for the past, appear to have moved backwards from early positive attitudes to the outcome of the 1994 elections, into defensive attitudes of denial and isolation.

Can there be any comparison between such attitudes and those illustrated in Rudyard Kipling's 1899 poem? 'Take up the White Man's Burden,' he wrote, 'to seek another's profit, and work another's gain ... And when your goal is nearest, the end for others sought, watch sloth and heathen folly bring all your hopes to nought'. More than a hundred years later, do such attitudes of cultural and racially defined superiority still exist?

It is apparent that, among those who choose to isolate themselves from the lives of the majority of South Africans, there are some who harbour racist and ignorant views about the state of present-day society, who criticise corruption and inefficiency as if these were racially defined characteristics, and who seek to safeguard their privileges and remain unaffected by the problems of those around them. Certainly, reading many of the letters written by bigots to the editors of newspapers, or listening to some radio discussions, might offer one serious cause to despair.

Yet these are the views of a vocal minority. There are thousands of organisations and individuals who dedicate much of their lives to seeking ways of improving the lives of others. Charitable and welfare organisations, faith-based initiatives, professionals who give some or all of their time to voluntary service, non-profit organisations working for justice and socio-economic rights, intellectuals who study situations of injustice and need, and seek causes and possible remedies – all these ventures include white people who wish to contribute to a common society that is more just and equitable. The example set by the Restitution Foundation, led by Deon Snyman, and its work in Worcester, inspires hope in the capacity of people to change themselves and others, working painstakingly towards greater understanding and recognition of the value of acknowledgement and atonement.

The question that faces this section of South Africa's population is whether this is enough to bring about the transformation needed to achieve the removal of the gross inequalities that define society. As long ago as 1975, Sheena Duncan asked of a white audience: 'We talk of a shared society, but cling to the capitalist, free enterprise model, which has provided for us here so well. Can it provide for everyone else on the same scale? I do not know the answer but I would like to know that we were asking the question'. She continued to ask the hard questions about land, housing, transport and other services, and to point out that 'Some of us are bound by fear of change and of the future'. She sought to 'identify the chains which bind us' and to be freed of the burden of privilege and power (Hendrikz, 2015: 200–201).

Neither the processes of the TRC, nor efforts by well-intentioned white people, have the capacity to produce the freedom from that burden, although 'identifying the chains' can be a step forward. A major alteration in the relations of wealth, power and privilege is required to break those chains.

Samantha Vice (2010: 236) examines how 'the internal, very personal moral project' for whites to consider how to deal with their past and ongoing privilege might lead them to a stance of 'humility and silence', and argues that this would allow for listening to the voices of others instead of seeking to be heard.

Listening, and learning how to avoid dominating conversations and assuming a right to leadership, are critically important. Yet white South Africans have not only a right to speak out, but also a responsibility to participate in the task of dismantling inequality and building inclusivity. Their task is to understand and acknowledge the ways in which unequal relationships were constructed to their advantage, and to demonstrate their willingness to deconstruct them.

Neville Alexander, referring to the racism 'which is one of the fundamental structural features of the system that spawned the gross violations', cites Deborah Posel: 'If we don't understand the conditions under which racism was produced, reproduced and intensified in South Africa, taking account of its interconnectedness with other modes of power and inequality such as gender and class, how can we transcend it?' (Alexander, 2002: 124–125).

For the new generation, which barely remembers the TRC, understanding racism as one of the modes of power and inequality is still a vital focus. Alexander was prescient in arguing that 'the contribution of the TRC to "reconciliation" in South Africa is a very limited one. It is clear that the main impetus for reconciliation will come from the economic and the educational sectors' (Alexander, 2002: 135).

Events at South African universities during the current year, and especially since the student bodies rallied around the call in October to support the #FeesMustFall campaign, have demonstrated how far the country is from reconciliation, and how the issues of racism and economic inequality have continued to foment alienation. Even before the #RhodesMustFall confrontations at the University of Cape Town, there were voices being raised at various institutions about the need to address the content of the curriculum, about racist attitudes experienced by black students, about the extent of the burden of student debt, and about the lack of transformation of the academic staff.

The generation of the parents of these students is dramatically reminded of the 1970s, the influence of the Black Consciousness Movement and the leadership of Steve Biko and his associates. The breakaway of black students from the National Union of South African Students (NUSAS) and the formation of the South African Students Organisation (SASO), gave birth to a new awareness in many circles. The crackdown of the apartheid security system over the Soweto students' protests in 1976 and then the killing of Biko in 1977, demonstrated the full extent of the power of the state. Yet, at the same time the philosophy of black consciousness had a powerful impact on the thinking of white South Africans who had been committed to bringing about change. This can be illustrated by referring to debates in academic and other structures – for example, the reports of the Study Project on Christianity in Apartheid Society (SPROCAS), and the teaching and writings of Rick Turner (assassinated in 1978).

Many of the parents who remember their own activism in the 1970s and 1980s have expressed their support for the current student demands and their protest actions. They include white parents, just as the protests have increasingly drawn in the support and participation of white students. The way in which the protests have spread rapidly around the country and the extent of their support have been remarkable. The decisions of the various institutions, and of the government, to accede to the demand for no increase in university fees for 2016, and to embark on the reversal of outsourcing the provision of services, have been a recognition of the seriousness of the campaign.

It is too early to discern whether this could be a movement that might break down divisions between privileged, mainly white, young people and the disadvantaged majority. But it is once again obliging white South Africans to consider their role in contributing to a reduction of inequality on all fronts. Education is the centre of the whirlwind of change at this time, but there are other storms brewing in the form of unemployment, unacceptable living conditions and extreme poverty. Those who are most affected will lead the movements for social justice, but there is work for white people to do: this will consist in the first instance of active listening, respect for the arguments of others, and a willingness to accept change. We should not leave the universities unsupported as they deal with the new provisions for fees. We should use what influence and power we do have to enable change to happen, not to retard it.

The change that is required is enormous and means facing up to measures required to reduce or remove that 'intolerable gap' of which the TRC spoke. A national development plan should include mechanisms to prevent exploitation and the extreme enrichment of those who are in the upper reaches of the economy. We have many tools and a great deal of information about poverty and its causes and effects, but are reluctant to put these into action for fear of damaging investment. Yet the greatest investment we could make, and one that is in the interests of the wealthy as well as the poor, would be to build a more equitable and less fractured society.

The white person's burden today is not guilt, not leadership, but acknowledgement of past and on-going privilege; and the resultant responsibility to accept radical change and to participate in developing a more inclusive society.

References

Alexander, N. (2002) *An Ordinary Country*. Pietermaritzburg: University of Natal Press.
Hendrikz, A. (2015) *Sheena Duncan*. Cape Town: Tiber Tree Press.
Matthews, S. (2010) 'Differing interpretations of reconciliation in South Africa'. *Transformation* 74.
Truth and Reconciliation Commission. *Report*: Volumes 1–5, 1998; Volumes 6–7, 2003.

Vice, S. (2010) 'How do I live in this strange place?' *Journal of Social Philosophy* 41(3).

'The White Man's Burden'. This poem, together with various interpretations and criticisms, can be found at https://en.wikipedia.org/wiki/The_White_Man%27s_Burden.

Appendix

The White Man's Burden

Original title: 'The White Man's Burden: The United States and the Philippine Islands', published 1899.

Take up the White Man's burden— Send forth the best ye breed—
Go bind your sons to exile To serve your captives' need;
To wait in heavy harness, On fluttered folk and wild—
Your new-caught, sullen peoples, Half-devil and half-child.

Take up the White Man's burden— In patience to abide,
To veil the threat of terror And check the show of pride;
By open speech and simple, An hundred times made plain,
To seek another's profit, And work another's gain.

Take up the White Man's burden— The savage wars of peace—
Fill full the mouth of Famine And bid the sickness cease;
And when your goal is nearest The end for others sought,
Watch sloth and heathen Folly Bring all your hopes to nought.

Take up the White Man's burden— No tawdry rule of kings,
But toll of serf and sweeper— The tale of common things,
The ports ye shall not enter, The roads ye shall not tread,
Go mark them with your living, And mark them with your dead.

Take up the White Man's burden— And reap his old reward:
The blame of those ye better, The hate of those ye guard—
The cry of hosts ye humour (Ah, slowly!) toward the light:—
'Why brought he us from bondage, Our loved Egyptian night?'

Take up the White Man's burden— Ye dare not stoop to less—
Nor call too loud on Freedom To cloke your weariness;
By all ye cry or whisper, By all ye leave or do,
The silent, sullen peoples Shall weigh your gods and you.

Take up the White Man's burden— Have done with childish days—
The lightly proffered laurel, The easy ungrudged praise.
Comes now, to search your manhood, through all the thankless years,
Cold, edged with dear-bought wisdom, The judgment of your peers!

White power today

CHRISTI VAN DER WESTHUIZEN

It is absolutely necessary work to disturb whiteness by making it seen, as it derives its power from operating invisibly as an unspoken regime of oppressive norms. Whiteness is therefore not skin pigmentation, but the meaning attached to pinkish, white-ish skin. A hierarchy of human value is created, which normalises people with such skin as naturally belonging to the top; while darker skinned people are racialised as black, to be placed as naturally at the bottom. The symbolic naturalisation of white superiority has a material effect, in the form of white privilege and black deprivation.

While apartheid has officially come to an end, white power persists, symbolically and materially.

Democracy has been good to white people in South Africa, including economically, judging by their increased wealth. The average annual income in white households was R125,495 in 1996 – in contrast to the average annual income in black households, at R29,827. White income rose to R530,880 in 2013, in contrast to black income rising to R88,327. In 2008, the 20 per cent at the top of the income pyramid consisted of 83 per cent of white people (3.7 million individuals), as opposed to only 11 per cent of African people (4.4 million individuals), 25 per cent of coloured people (1.1 million individuals) and 60 per cent of Indian people (740,000 individuals) (Leibbrandt and Woolard in Terreblanche, 2012). Black South

Africans (23.7 million individuals) constitute the overwhelming majority of the poorest half of the population, with coloured South Africans (1.3 million individuals) making up the balance.

White poverty, historically an Afrikaner phenomenon, remains a mere sliver of overall poverty. In 2011, with reference to the apartheid population categories, a mere 0.8 per cent of white people lived in poverty, compared to 54 per cent of African people, 27.6 per cent of coloured people and 3.4 per cent of Indian people (Statistics SA, 2014: 27). This was not always the case for Afrikaans-speaking whites. The poor white problem, as it was called, looms large in the history of this group. But this problem has been all but eradicated. Apartheid was an effective affirmative action scheme, if we look at the figures. Afrikaner-controlled companies on the Johannesburg Stock Exchange (JSE) increased from zero in 1948 to just less than 10 per cent in the late 1970s; to 20 per cent by 1990; to 24 per cent in 1996; and 35 per cent in 2000 (Laurence, 2000; Van der Westhuizen, 2007).

Along with other factors, the so-called poor white problem provided the fodder for Afrikaner nationalist invention. Coloureds, liberals and socialists were purged, and the nascent racial feminists were domesticated. What remained was cobbled together as an Afrikaner identity.

Allow me to stand still at this point and say a few words about how Afrikaner identity was historically formed. All identities are forged through exclusions, and Afrikaner identity is no exception in that respect. However, the set of discourses mobilised under the moniker Afrikaner consists of particular elements that are relevant to the specific form apartheid took. As Afrikaner nationalism constituted an identity in opposition to liberals, socialists and African nationalists, it created the disciplinary mechanism of *volksvreemdheid* – literally 'strange to the people' – in which *andersdenkendheid* – 'thinking differently' – was penalised. This demand of conformism was fortified by the fascist strand that developed through the Ossewa Brandwag (Oxwagon Sentinel), which was absorbed into the NP after Germany's defeat in World War II. From that fascist strand, Balthazar John Vorster emerged as justice minister to institute detention without trial, after which he was promoted to prime minister, replacing the assassinated

Hendrik Frensch Verwoerd in the mid-1960s. As the heaviest penalty was meted out to black outsiders, those from within who dared to resist, who dared to be *volksvreemd*, paid high prices and sometimes the highest price. It was in the Vorster era that a very ill Bram Fischer was kept in prison almost right up to his death, the same era in which Breyten Breytenbach was locked up after his radicalisation due to the racism against his partner. It was in the Vorster era that Ingrid Jonker was publicly maligned and ended her life by walking into the sea at Three Anchor Bay. The Vorster era was the height of apartheid hegemony, when this culture of *eendersdenkendheid* – 'thinking the same' – was at its peak. But the hegemony started slipping just as it was at its height in the mid-1960s. The *verligtes* (or more liberally minded Afrikaners) had developed moral doubts about apartheid, while the capitalists among them were worried that apartheid had become a constraint rather than an aid to profitability, as it had been previously. The *verligtes* commenced the reform of apartheid, largely in the form of the attempted co-option of certain groups of black people. In response, the *verkramptes* split away to pursue the return of Verwoerdian apartheid.

The *eendersdenkendheid* that underpinned Afrikaner nationalism is not amenable to democracy. The question is: what are Afrikaans white people doing with our newfound democracy and renewed prosperity? Fortunately, the picture is varied. I identify three groupings: the Afrikaans African nationalists, the neo-Afrikaner or Afrikaans enclave nationalists, and the Afrikaans South Africans.

The most clearly identifiable Afrikaner nationalists, the former NP rulers, have merged with the currently ruling African nationalists, as I discuss at length in my book *White Power*, where they have made their – what shall we call it? – *talents* felt in ANC entities such as the Progressive Business Forum. They are the Afrikaans African nationalists.

The second grouping is the neo-Afrikaner enclave nationalists. They are currently the most vocal, and are therefore frequently positioned by other South Africans as 'the' Afrikaners, as if they are wholly representative. Therefore, it is worth discussing them in greater detail. We are seeing the worst elements that marked Afrikaner culture in its constitutive phase in the first half of the twentieth century being dug up like an old cow from a ditch – to use an Afrikaans expression – a cow that has been stuffed and presented as though it is brand new.

The enclave nationalists include organised neo-Afrikaner nationalist remnants to the far right, the so-called *verkramptes*, who refocus their efforts on reactivating the hierarchies and inequalities that had historically produced, maintained and refurbished apartheid. Simultaneously, these remnants avail themselves of the reconnection of South Africa into global circuits of knowledge to draw on neo-liberalism, neo-racism, neo-sexism and the postmodern 'return to the local' to legitimise and reupholster their enclave nationalism. In an unexpected manoeuvre, we see the convergence of the *verligtes* and the *verkramptes*. *Verligtes* harvest the fruits of neo-liberal access and affluence but increasingly turn towards the *verkramptes*' vision of enclave nationalism to find identity anchors amid the postcolonial tumult.

The enclave nationalists' whiteness looks to the Global North for guidance, as their antecedents did. The globally dominant Anglo-American rationality of neo-liberalism is articulated with remnants of Afrikaner nationalism to infuse these remains with a new lease on life. This happens less in Orania than in geographically specific suburban sites in our big cities. This whiteness constructs its own version of Stuart Hall's 'the return to the local', which I call inward migration. This inward migration is to class-based territories with very specific versions of sexuality, gender and race that create an exclusive and excluding ethnic configuration.

Enclave nationalism hinges on the basic precept of capitalism – private property – and is enabled by the wholesale privatisation and monetisation of life under neo-liberalism. Individuals become Afrikaners by being consumers of Afrikaner culture, spaces and anti-politics. Afrikaner identity is enacted through consumption. In this regard, Solidariteit and AfriForum have stepped forward as the masters of the trade in Afrikaner identity, the twenty-first century versions of the cultural entrepreneurs who first cobbled together the Afrikaner a century ago. In the contemporary context, politics is stigmatised as pursued by backward people. Afrikaner politics is recast in the guise of an anti-politics channelled through the consumption of products ranging from financial services to education, security and labour.

The place where the *verligtes* and the *verkramptes* meet is under the sign of consumption. As was the case with Afrikaner nationalism, *die taal* (the language) is central. You make your retreat into your white Afrikaans world through the plethora of Afrikaner cultural products spawned by reinvented neo-liberal Afrikaner organisations, from the media to cultural industries to trade unions. So we have seen a wholesale neo-liberalisation of Afrikaner identity that was ripe for articulation in the wake of the rupture in Afrikaner nationalism's grip on these individuals.

From the Global North the enclave version of Afrikaans whiteness draws the lessons of reinventing racism as culture, and heterosexism as family values. Enclave nationalists make cultural claims with which they set themselves apart from the dominant Anglo whiteness. This emphasis historically under apartheid included dividing people racialised as black into multiple ethnic others, hence the bantustans. From there it is a short step to deploy the strategy of reworking and reupholstering racism as culture. The Afrikaner claim on an unchanging Afrikaner ethnic essence, transmitted through culture, is projected onto multiple ethnic black others to validate its ethnic claim on Afrikanerness. It is a claim to effect separateness. Here we see the spectre of apartheid reappearing. This ethnic separateness actualises racial separation, aiding the maintenance of this group's ill-begotten privilege, which flies in the face of contemporary South Africa's ethical imperative of redistribution.

The family values trope, used across the globe to attempt to roll back the gains of feminism and queer movements, has been analysed as a centrepiece of new racism. But it has also been pointed out that the family was centrally placed in colonial racisms and of pivotal ideological and organisational importance. The Afrikaner nationalist version serves as an example. While we dismantle the racial organisation of apartheid, we must also dismantle the internal repressions of gendered and sexualised others. The internal division is as highly hierarchical as the external division and reflects the external division in ways that draw on colonial inter-sectionalities. Particularist practices of race, gender, sexuality and class are elaborated in spaces of commerce and religion, or spaces in which commerce and religion are conflated and which provide institutional bases for the elaboration of these practices. Apart from family and church, educational institutions are also utilised. Schools and universities are sites for what I call racialised heteronormativity, passed off as Afrikaans or Afrikaner culture.

Last, like Afrikaner nationalism, its renewed enclave version expediently switches between race and ethnicity to safeguard its position of supremacy. When it suits, it submerges itself in dominant Anglo whiteness to demand the latter's privileges: for example, C.J. Rhodes as a symbol of whiteness and white masculine (not homosexual, of course!) achievement. It also claims colour blindness, in an embrace of that tried and tested strategy of Anglo whiteness. But at other times, when it suits, it claims its specificity and its threatened status as a minority, for example on university campuses. These are the workings of whiteness, as exposed by #RhodesMustFall and other student actions. It shows the pervasiveness and the hold on identities of the culture of whiteness in South Africa today, bringing research findings into mainstream discourses, particularly the post-apartheid innovation in which institutional spaces are used to demand that apartheid's others accede to whiteness masquerading as 'standards' and normalised as 'the way we do things here'.

In contrast, my research also shows Afrikaans white individuals who refuse attempts to interpolate them into neo-Afrikaner enclave nationalism. These people belong to the third group, the Afrikaans South Africans. I have investigated post-apartheid identity formation among individuals who identify as heterosexual, middle-class, white and female. Some identify as Afrikaners, while others don't. They are engaged in practices of continuous critical reflection on the racism and sexism inherent to Afrikaner nationalism and work actively against it in their family contexts and in their own positioning in racial and gender relations. They recognise that their privilege is due to their positioning as white in the racist organisation of apartheid. They also recognise how their ethno-racial positioning previously allowed them to ameliorate their secondary status as women. They acknowledge and resist the intra-Afrikaner mode of gendering. They reinvent their senses of self and agency, drawing on complex mélanges of democratic and feminist egalitarianism, and Afrikaner nationalist symbolism. Most interesting is the re-working of the best of their cultural legacy – the hard-working, tenacious *volksmoeder* (mother of the nation) – to shed its patriarchal racism and redirect its values to advance an ethical life. They are feminist *volksmoeders* creating new ways of being to unlock their own and others' potential for an inclusive humanity based on social justice.

References

Laurence, P. (2000) 'Black-led companies struggle as Afrikaner strength pushes on'. *Irish Times* 3 March.
Statistics SA. (2014) *Poverty Trends in South Africa 2006–2011: An Examination of Absolute Poverty Between 2006 and 2011*. Pretoria: Statistics SA.
Terreblanche, S. (2012) *Lost in Transformation: South Africa's Search for a New Future Since 1986*. Johannesburg: KMM Review Publishing.
Van der Westhuizen, C. (2007) *White Power and the Rise and Fall of the National Party*. Cape Town: Zebra Press.

Whiteness and the South African Economy

Capitalism, racialism and whiteness

LYNETTE STEENVELD

As this session focuses on 'Whiteness and the South African Economy', I will direct my comments to probing the relationship between whiteness as a constructed social identity which conjures warm bodies with histories, cultures, values, etc.; and the economy which may be more abstract, but is still the outcome of the activities of warm bodies, and it too has a history.

My starting point is the acknowledgement that the South African economy is a capitalist one. As Michael Burawoy has noted, in order 'to understand the differential access of races to resources requires a theory of the more general allocation of resources, which in turn presupposes a theory of capitalism' (1981: 280). His argument, broadly, is that if we are to understand racialism and racism, then we need to see it not as a given, but need to enquire into its origins. From his perspective, this necessitates theorising the position of different racial groups in relation to particular capitalist social structures, so that one can better understand 'the different forms of race relations and racial antagonisms that are subsumed under the single overweening formula of "racism"' (1981: ibid.) On this basis he argues that 'no longer does one have few resources because one is black; instead one is black because one has few resources' (1981: ibid.) In other words, he sees the construction of identities and ideologies in relation to an economic social system, in this case a capitalist one, in which different groups – both capitalists and sections of labour – position themselves, at different moments and in relation to different tensions, in order to maintain the system as a whole. The state is the outcome of this system, 'presenting in its very structure the organizational power of the capitalist class' (1981: 288). Burawoy explains further: 'The state, using Gramsci's metaphor, can be understood as a system of trenches which contain and organize the struggles among and within classes in ways that do not threaten the capitalist order' (1981: ibid.)

It is within this general theoretical context that the racialisation of South African society can be understood, and with it, the different roles played by the state, segments of capital, and segments of labour. Neither capital nor labour has a singular identity, but rather is produced by the economic and social tensions between and within them in relation to the changing nature of the state.

The history of South Africa from colonial times is an anti-colonial struggle of the indigenous population against European economic expansionism. Thus whiteness and the economy can most simply be understood in terms of the waves of European settlement from Jan van Riebeeck in 1652 to the present time. The resources fought over were always economic ones – whether among the colonising settlers themselves (Dutch and English); or between various kinds of coalition between colonists and the indigenous people. The kinds of economic development and the nature of the state changed and is well documented. At a political level, Mahmood Mamdani's *Citizen and Subject* (1996) is an insightful account of the political engagement between colonisers and colonised, through which the colonisers became citizens accorded the status of races while the colonised became ethnic subjects. One of the political struggles of indigenous peoples was thus to become citizens in their own countries.

On the economic front, in the nineteenth century mining and later industrial development depended on various forms of state policy to ensure the sustainability of the whole system of capitalist development, which was an extension of global capitalism. Initially segregation enforced the discontinuous (dual/split) labour market that created two labour markets, one white (coloniser) and rich, the other black (indigenous) and poor (Burawoy, 1981; Adler and Webster, 1995: 77–83). From 1948, apartheid served a similar purpose.

Tracking the history of labour struggles and the development of trade unionism in South Africa is an instructive way of making sense of the complex relations between labour, capital and the state, and the ways in which race and ethnicity were produced and reproduced through these processes (Roux, 1948, 1964). As Adler and Webster note:

White workers dominated the trade union movement. Their historical privileges, entrenched through their craft unions established at the turn of the century, made them something of a labour aristocracy. The organization of Black workers occurred through bodies subordinated to White unions or through highly vulnerable independent organizations under left-wing leadership on the periphery of the official labor movement (1995: 78).

An iconic example of the complexity of these relations is the 1922 Rand Rebellion, where one section of the working class, the commandoes of Fordsburg, marched with the infamous banner 'Workers of the World, Unite and Fight for a White South Africa'. On the ground we saw the conflicts between different sectors of labour (skilled, unskilled, British immigrant, Afrikaner, African, coloured), based on their understanding of what the key struggle against the mining houses should be, while from the air white miners were attacked by the state in its attempts to contain the revolt (Roux, 1948, 1964).

Another key moment in the more recent history of this struggle was the emergence of black worker activity which surfaced in Durban in 1973. According to Adler and Webster:

The slow emergence of non-racial industrial unions during the 1970s challenged the comfortable 'social contract' between the apartheid state, employers, and White labor based on protectionism and cheap Black labor. By the 1970s the official

> (White) labor movement was a spent force, with falling membership and a rapidly declining ability to protect members' material interests. At the same time, Black workers began building the modern labor movement, organizing on a formally non-racial class basis, and soon displaced the racist unions as the institutional center of South African labor. (1995: 79)

The formation of the Federation of South African Trade Unions (FOSATU) in 1979 was significant in this process as it brought together the new industrial unions under one umbrella body. But it was only with the labour law reforms of the Wiehahn Commission (1977–1979) that black workers' trade union rights were legally recognised. Notwithstanding FOSATU's strategy to remain independent of political affiliation, it helped in the formation of the Congress of South African Trade Unions (COSATU) as a 'super-federation', which as we know aligned itself with the then banned ANC (Adler and Webster, 1995: 80).

The ANC, COSATU and the South African Communist Party (SACP) are historical descendants of early union and political organisations formed to challenge the colonial usurpation of both the economy and the state. The triple alliance between the ANC, COSATU and the SACP also signalled the post-1994 politico-economic desire to address the inequalities of the past. Economically this was expressed by the ANC government's 1994 economic policy, the Reconstruction and Development Programme (RDP). Despite its promise of economic and social redress, 'In the end the RDP reflected an uneasy compromise between "the feasibility of combining a social and welfare state in the developmental sphere with neo-liberalism in the economic sphere"' (Padayachee and Sherbut, 2007: 30, citing Bond, 2000: 54). This was followed in 1996 by the Growth, Employment and Redistribution (GEAR) strategy which has been roundly criticised by COSATU and others. As Padayachee and Sherbut note, 'Adelzadeh (1996) has argued that the model used was in fact that of the South African Reserve Bank, which was used to underpin the apartheid regime's neo-liberal Normative Economic Model' (2007: 31, citing Adelzadeh, 1996: 70). What this points to is the economic continuities between the object of anti-colonial struggles that culminated in apartheid as the most recent form of state to protect capitalism, and the contemporary ANC-led government's economic policies, despite it having been one of the key organisations fighting for the 'liberation' of South Africa. It is also arguable that COSATU's alliance with a political party is no longer in the interests of the black working class.

It is within this larger, and global, context that 'Whiteness and the South African Economy' needs to be thought about. It is in this context that the rise and politics of Solidarity and AfriForum must be understood. And it is also in this context that the changing nature of capitalism and its relation to the South African state should be understood. We cannot theorise 'whiteness as a position of advantage' (Frankenberg, 1993) in South Africa without locating it in relation to the history of capitalist development and the struggles of working people against it, and the forms of state it engendered.

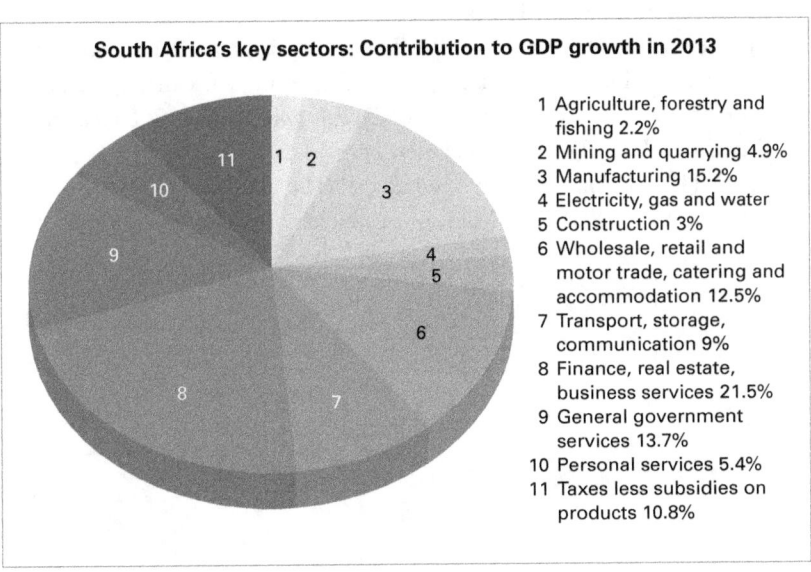

Source: Statistics South Africa
http://www.mediaclubsouthafrica.com/component/content/article?id=111:sa-economy-key-sectors

References

Adelzadeh, A. (1996) 'From the RDP to GEAR: the gradual embracing of neo-liberalism in economic policy'. *Transformation* 31.

Adler, G. and Webster, E. (1995) 'Challenging transition theory: the labour movement, radical reform and the transition to democracy in South Africa'. *Politics and Society* 23(1): 75–106.

Bond, P. (2000) *Elite Transition: From Apartheid to Neo-Liberalism in South Africa*. Pietermaritzburg: University of Natal Press.

Burawoy, M. (1981) 'The capitalist state in South Africa: Marxist and sociological perspectives on race and class'. *Political Power and Social Theory* 2: 279–335.

Frankenberg, R. (1993) *White Women, Race Matters: The Social Construction of Whiteness*. Minneapolis: University of Minnesota Press.

Mamdani, M. (1996) *Citizen and Subject: Contemporary Africa and the Legacy of Late Colonialism*. Kampala: Fountain Publishers; Cape Town: David Philip; London: James Currey.

Padayachee, V. and Sherbut, G. (2007) 'Ideas and power: academic economists and the making of economic policy: the South African experience in comparative perspective'. *School of Development Studies, University of KwaZulu-Natal, Durban Working Paper* 43.

Roux, E. (1948) *Time Longer than Rope: The Black Man's Struggle for Freedom in South Africa*. Madison: University of Wisconsin Press.

The colour of capital

BOBBY GODSELL

Introduction

Before turning to the subject I have been asked to address, I would like to record four convictions with regard to the concept of race, a concept clearly central to today's round-table.
1. Race clearly is and will continue to be a powerful shaper of social identities, and an agent in the exercise of power and wealth in South Africa.
2. Race will continue to play these roles both in competition and combination with other patterns of social meaning such as language, culture, class, ideology and religious belief.
3. Race can never be a reason to deny the shared humanity and equality of respect, rights, responsibilities and opportunities that are the birthright of each individual South African.
4. As we move into the third decade of our young democracy, we can neither ignore race, nor absolutise its claims on our national values.

Turning to my topic

I have been asked to address the colour of capitalism. You may conclude that I will talk as much about the character of contemporary capitalism as its colour. Hopefully, I will do so in a way that examines meaningfully the way race has shaped wealth and power in our country's past, and continues to do so.

Our settler colonialism and its organisation of wealth and power

I want to remind us of the way in which assets, professions and networks worked in apartheid South Africa.

From the arrival of the first colonial settlers, even with Van Riebeeck's hedge, land was increasingly reserved for the economic use and benefit of whites. This applied over time to the ownership and control of other categories of assets. Professions (and here I use the term broadly to include managers) were also the dominant preserve of white South Africans. Finally, the networks through which individuals gained access to capital, skills and leadership roles in the economy were fundamentally white in nature.

This pattern of race-defined access to both power and wealth is not only a stain on our history, it remains a dynamic force shaping both our present and future.

The way it does this is very well illustrated by the reality of South Africa's universities – a reality so dramatically presented to all who can see and hear by tens of thousands of both brave and deeply patriotic young South Africans. Since 1994, enrolment in our universities has doubled to more than one million students. Using the numbers available for 2012 in a Department of Higher Education and Training (DHET) report some 67 per cent of the 'contact' students are black South Africans and 20 per cent are white; 54 per cent female and 46 per cent male. In the case of distance learners these ratios are 73 per cent black, 15 per cent white, 64 per cent female and 36 per cent male. Surely these numbers indicate a great achievement of non-racial, non-sexist and democratic South Africa.

Yet the events of recent weeks have made us aware that achieving access to university does not guarantee effective teaching and learning. This has also been our experience with both primary and secondary schooling. Nor should these problems surprise us.

Most of the new entrants to our universities come from poor households and communities. These 'first in a generation' students lack many of the attributes needed to complete university studies successfully. They lack financial resources. The experience of an organisation that has managed large numbers of undergraduate bursaries for more than four decades suggests that poor students need bursaries of at least R100,000 per year to meet the basic necessities of study. Yet the state student loan is significantly less than this. Student hunger is a reality in our corridors of learning: Gift of the Givers apparently regularly feeds 2,000 students at the University of Johannesburg. Poor students battle to find suitable accommodation (and, it should be noted, not all university residences provide accommodation that facilitates effective study). Poor students rely on public transport, which makes late classes and field study difficult. Poor students often lack digital access.

Our universities are simply not equipped to teach well such resource-poor students.

It is an immense achievement of those young South Africans who lead university protests across our land that these issues are now squarely on the table. This agenda demands a constructive response from every sector of South African society, including business.

I have used the university as a prism to illustrate a race legacy that makes hollow the promises of our Constitution and Bill of Rights. If economic transformation means anything surely it must mean the honest, direct and effective addressing of these challenges.

The new capitalism

It is deeply ironic that, just as the apartheid edifice began to crumble in the 1980s, so too a quite new form of capitalism began to emerge in the global community to which South Africa would return a decade later.

This new capitalism can be described in many ways. Industrial economies disappeared and were replaced by a services-dominated (often financial services) economy. Workers became consumers. Growth became consumption-driven, not production-driven. Larger and larger proportions of economic growth became debt or credit funded.

The deepest changes were to be seen in the patterns of capital accumulation and also in the role of the firm, company or corporation. Whereas in earlier stages of industrial society, capital or investment was dominantly the activity of the rich, from the middle of the twentieth century the contractual savings of working people have become the dominant source of investment. Initially, both pensions and life insurance were housed in trusts and societies, and were managed with conservative mandates that measured performance precisely over the lifetime this financial product was meant to serve. This conservatism was often enforced by government policy prescriptions that required these kinds of savings to be invested in safe and secure instruments such as government bonds. The deregulation and individualisation of employee pension savings started by Margaret Thatcher, and closely followed by Ronald Reagan, and which has now become a global norm, changed all this. This massive savings flow was now free to be invested in pretty much the complete range of investment products, including many that were quite new. Individual employees were entitled to regular (often three-monthly) reports on the performance of these funds. With the introduction of personal employee pension plans (PEPS in the UK) and their 401(k) equivalent in the USA, the individual employee could manage his own investments.

A similar pattern of change occurred with life insurance, the other most common working-class instrument of savings. With the demutualisation of life insurance companies, these mutual societies, in which those who lived contributed to the benefits of those who died, became (generally) listed companies with shareholders who expected to earn significant returns.

These two changes in the character of capital required a new breed of manager – the fund manager. This new manager is charged with the allocation, acquisition and disposal of investment instruments for the monthly massive inflows of contractual savings. They win the right to do this through their performance record. This performance is typically measured three monthly.

Let us now consider the changes in the role of firm, company or corporation. In the first phase of industrialisation all over the world, the first great companies had a family nature. This was the time of the Rockefellers, Morgans, Mellons and Fords in America and of course the Oppenheimers, Ruperts and Wessels here in South Africa. As these companies grew in both size and ambition, so families turned to the public to raise additional capital. Companies became publicly listed and were governed by a board of directors increasingly independent of the original founders.

Now, however, we have entered a third phase: companies now compete for funds from fund managers. These fund managers have more influence over their strategies, performance and character than do either the original founders or the boards. Funds with significant stakes (often as little as 10 per cent) can effectively fire chief executives and board chairs.

For example, when a major company gets into trouble today (let's take MTN as an example) it is more likely to be called to account by a large institutional investor (or fund manager) such as the Public Investment Corporation, with its one trillion Rand of invested funds, than its founders or board. (The PIC today probably owns more of the JSE than Anglo ever did.)

What is the significance of this new capitalism in relation to dealing with our country's legacy of a racial past?

Deputy Minister Nel asked provocatively: where are the Suzmans, Slovos, Fischers and Naudés of today? With a view more narrowly to economic transformation I would rephrase this question: who are the Oppenheimers, Rosholts, Ruperts and Wessels of 2015?

Our economy is a small ship floating on a global sea. We can neither ignore nor defy fund manager capitalism. And indeed, this much more diverse, much more metric-driven pattern of economic direction has enhanced transparency and (sometimes) improved efficiencies. Yet the behaviour of fund managers (driven one must acknowledge by the competitive greed of their investing clients) has made economic and social goals, which must be addressed over years and decades, difficult to address. Also, it has isolated risk and return in a way that earlier industrial barons would find almost mindless. So, as I attempted to attract these new fund manager captains of capitalism into holding AngloGold shares, I would have to address their fear of political instability, fed at least in part by continuing poverty. On the other hand, if I were to report a reduction in wage costs through retrenchments, this would be viewed by the same managers as a plus. The trade-offs of nation formation (and company building for that matter) do not rate well in fund manager metrics.

Of course, among fund managers there are many who think longer term. And there are those who look for investments where stability, sustainability and even social justice are required. These are the things demanded by the social and ethics committees provided by the boards of companies in terms of South Africa's new and highly progressive Companies Act of 2008.

We need this character in our economic leaders – those who direct investment, such as the fund managers; the boards of our companies, to whom the executive managements are accountable; trade union leaders; and, indeed, leaders in broader society – if we are to address those challenges identified in MISTRA's *Nation Formation and Social Cohesion* report. This includes achieving societal consensus on a decent standard of living and the values system that should characterise our workplaces.

Fortunately, South Africa is not alone in its concern about social cohesion and social justice. In the wake of the 2008 financial collapse, leaders from all sectors of society and in many countries are looking for growth that is more inclusive and fair.

I hope I have indicated that it will be the character of capital in 2016 and beyond, more than its colour, that will determine whether this market economy can also produce a fair society and a sustainable democracy.

Dear Mother Africa

DIRK HERMANN

I'm writing this letter to you, but I can't give it to you. This is just my story. It is not a complete story, but it is mine. In this story, I am not trying to tell my brothers' story. My other brothers have stories, too, sad stories of suffering and, put together, all our stories form our family story.

I hide the story in the back of my Bible as the other children would bully me when I express how I feel. I do feel better, though, when writing it down.

Mother, why am I your discarded child? I look different and I talk differently. Another mother has influenced me but that's not my mother.

I was born of you, Mother Africa, a child of Africa. I have been here on the southern tip of your home for eleven generations. I ask my brothers which of them can list the names of eleven generations that have lived here in the South. They can't, yet they call me the stranger.

Soon after 1652, the first Vryburgers (Free Burghers) turned their backs on Europe and turned their faces towards Africa. That is how my birth, that of the Afrikaner, started. It was a painful birth filled with suffering and sorrow, but I called myself after you Mother, I called myself 'Afrikaner'. Afrikaner. My speech developed, and a language emerged, which I called after you, Mother. I called it Afrikaans. I wanted to be free in Africa. In 1707, Hendrik Biebouw said: 'Ik ben een africaander – Ik wil niet loopen, 'k ben een africaander al slaan die landdrost mijn dood of al setten hij mijn in de tronk'. (I am an Afrikaander – I don't want to go away. I am an Afrikaander even if the magistrate beats me to death or throws me into jail.)

Mother, I didn't want to be subservient to European colonialists; 'ek bin een Africaander', and I moved deeper into Africa. I didn't move back, I moved in. My trek for a place in Africa. My brothers, too, migrated for a place in Africa.

Brother fought against brother for a place on the southern tip of Africa. Millions had to flee and hundreds of thousands were killed; some sources estimate the death toll to be between one and two million. Our home here on the southernmost tip of Africa was destabilised. Some of our brothers, like the Sothos, the Matebeles and the Tswanas, had to flee. Today, we still see the structural consequences of those times, such as Swaziland, Lesotho and Zimbabwe.

The women and children of some of our other brothers were taken by the stronger ones, their men killed. Shaka was the great warrior and today statues are erected in honour of him. I was part of those migratory patterns, I was looking for a place in Africa. I played a small role amid the major violence and disruption. Moreover, I tried to reach agreements and sign treaties; and for this those who are a part of me, Piet Retief and his men, were brutally killed. My women and children were battered to death at Bloukrans and Moordspruit. Some of my babies were tossed up into the air to fall onto spears when coming down. Why is that not a crime – could it be because I look different? I have also fought, conquered and lost, and like my other brothers I too have found a place in Africa.

But Mother, why do you build statues to honour the Mfecane of my other brothers, but I, I am the exploiter? Why is Shaka a freedom hero, but Piet Retief, the murdered one and other Voortrekkers are the ones who offend?

Why is that which was done to my other black brothers by black brothers not called a crime against humanity? Why is it acceptable that their women could be incorporated, the men killed and their land seized because it was done by black people? Why are you so patient when it comes to black on black violence?

Why is my quest for a place in Africa racism, but that of my brothers a justified quest? Why are you silent about certain parts of history while you emphasise others?

Again, I had to move, away from English colonialists, because 'Ik bin een Africaander'.

I settled in the North; in two republics – the Zuid-Afrikaansche Republiek (ZAR) and the Republic of the Orange Free State. The British colonialists, however, would not leave me alone. I fought the First Anglo-Boer War or First War of Freedom as an African tribe, and I became the first African tribe to defeat a colonial power. I built railway lines, and not only to the coast, to export wealth as the colonialists did in Africa. I used wealth to develop my place in Africa. I established mines and industries.

Then the colonialists wanted to colonise my mineral wealth and the Second Anglo-Boer War (the Second War of Freedom) started – an expensive and cruel war. It was the highest price yet paid for my place in Africa. My women and children were sent to concentration camps. About 34,000 of them died there. Around 30,000 of my men were exiled and farms were burnt to the ground. The war left 20,000 orphaned. My numbers were still relatively low and there was hardly a family of my kind not bereaved of a member. I had to pay a huge price for someone else's colonial ideals. Mother Africa, please don't ever again call me a colonialist, albeit a colonialist of a special kind, for it is an insult to me and to the graves of my ancestors.

Like typical colonialists, the English wanted to assimilate me after the war. They wanted to deprive me of Mother Africa to make me English. I had to wear a sign around my neck saying 'I am a donkey' when I spoke my African language. In spite of the government, we rose from the ashes. We started to establish community institutions. The Vrouefederasie addressed poverty, we founded educational and even economic institutions. We named our companies after South Africa, for example Sanlam, Santam, and we used indigenous names such as Volkskas and Federale Volksbeleggings; not colonial names such as Anglo American with one foot in England and the other in America while exploring Africa and exporting from here.

Again, we did not accept the colonialists' language, but preferred our own African language. Drought, the Depression and poverty hit me hard. It was my conviction that to rise out of poverty I had to be culturally rich and during those times of suffering the Bible was translated into Afrikaans; Afrikaans became an official language; and the Afrikaans Taal en Kultuurvereniging, the Federasie van Afrikaanse Kultuurveregings, the Afrikanerbond, Voortrekkers and so forth were established. And so Afrikaans became part of my identity as someone who is able to rebound. Not only do I speak Afrikaans, I am Afrikaans. Afrikaans became my language of aspiration and through the medium of Afrikaans I became modernised.

The price of war was very high, though. It made me suffer from the 'never again' syndrome. The children of apartheid still experienced the aftermath of the war's camps of death in their homes. Apartheid is not that simple but 'never again' had a huge influence.

Apartheid is a South African paradox. In reaction to the pain of colonialism, the logic of colonialism was pursued through apartheid – a central idea and system imposed from above. The price I, as an Afrikaner, had to pay for apartheid is that I lost my sense of community in exchange for subservience to a state system. Afrikaners became highly efficient civil servants, but the English, who to a large extent were outside the system, were more entrepreneurial and began to dominate the economy.

The apartheid system was unsustainable, discriminatory and humiliating. It led to a struggle for freedom from the system.

I am deeply conscious of my historical mistakes, especially during the time of apartheid. The mere emotion that goes through me when I think that my kids wouldn't be allowed to sit on certain benches or swing on certain swings gives me an inkling of the strong emotions my brothers must have experienced during those times.

Mother, you speak out against apartheid and you uphold the offender/victim relationship. You put me in a permanent position of guilt and you make sure it is kept like that.

You produce films and documentaries, write books and do many other things to make sure this offender/victim relationship remains in place. I am told that I should keep quiet because my debt to my brothers has not yet been settled and until that has happened I cannot claim my rights. You decreed me to moral silence.

But Mother, do you have a historical conscience for other abuses that took place here on the southernmost tip of Africa? Are you filled by remorse because of it and do you expect your children to apologise for it as Prince Buthelezi did by way of exception when he apologised for the murder of Piet Retief?

Why are you silent about the injustices done to my black brothers by black brothers during the struggle times? Why do the 200 people who were necklaced during one year not form part of the main narrative? Why are the councillors, Inkatha members and many others who were killed and burned to death not part of the main narrative? Why are you silent on the sorrow of my black brothers? By your silence you are normalising violence.

Mother, today I again hear 'never again'. I hear about a system that must free my brothers and restore them. I hear my brothers want to break free from the bondage of one system by becoming enslaved to another.

Mother, this brings me to the next paradox. I teach my children – and they hear it everywhere – that the system is not going to help you. You have to work hard and study diligently: 'White children, you are on your own.' In an ironic way they, unlike the children of apartheid, are free from the system. They are experiencing discrimination by a system, but they are not enslaved to it. Freedom from a system creates entrepreneurship. They will be like submerged corks that bounce back to the surface. As a result, government officials will ask: where do all the white people come from? There must still be discrimination in the system. Let's implement even more systems, impose higher fines and appoint more inspectors. The subheading of this strategy reads: let's make our people even more dependent on the system, because never again ...

Mother Africa, it would seem as if your children are perpetuating the 'never again' fallacy of the apartheid generation. In an attempt to redress a previous dispensation, the logic of that system is being persevered with. A great central idea, system and state (or empire) and all have to fit in. That logic will not bring about redress and will not deliver people. It will, frankly, not achieve what needs to happen and what it sets out to achieve.

What astonishes me most is that you have made someone else's language your language of aspiration. You gave up on our own language. How can someone tell me: my language can't do it? In my world that means I can't do it.

In this way, you are going to lose your children; this makes them colonialists of a special type.

Mother Africa, my love for you is profound – your wide open spaces, your natural beauty, your climate, and your soil. I don't live on Africa's soil; I am the soil of Africa. I love your children, my brothers and sisters, and over the years a special bond has developed between us. The children in our home are different, we look different, we talk differently, do things differently but we have one thing in common – Mother Africa.

I cannot and I do not want to go anywhere else. I do not have a colonial motherland that would send planes when things go wrong here. That I have nowhere to go is my strongest weapon for survival.

Perhaps you should again hear it today, Mother: 'Ik ben een africaander – Ik wil niet loopen, 'k ben een africaander al slaan die landdrost mijn dood of al setten hij mijn in de tronk.'

You are also a harsh mother, and you have harsh stories to tell of minorities on African soil. Stories of black on black violence in other countries on your soil: Rwanda, Kenya, Nigeria, and closer to home, Matabeleland. Yet, Robert Mugabe receives the most applause at the presidential inauguration and Omar al-Bashir is helped to flee the country. You despise colonialism and you have a history of driving colonialists from your countries. I am not one; yet you call me one.

Mother Africa, I have embraced you, but I don't experience your embracing a white child. In your legislation, you don't include me in the definition of African; your narrative is a simple good/bad narrative. White is bad and black is good. You are saying all problems started the day I arrived. You marginalise me and are upset when I keep myself aside. The racism of your other children is seen as legitimate demands; but my legitimate demands are racism. You refer to me as 'them' and your other children you call 'us'. That makes me vulnerable for I am a visibly discredited minority.

Why is it so difficult for you to accept me as your child? Why do you see me as another woman's child who should be thankful for the goodwill and patience being shown to it in the Africa home?

Mother Africa, are you a racist mother?

This is my heart, my story, the heart I may not share, and you, Mother, won't hear its pain because it is safely put away in my Bible.

Double standards and black privilege
The new story of South Africa

ERNST ROETS

'Jews are dishonest thieves who steal other people's money.'

'Asians are inhumane and they don't care for their fellow human beings.'

'Muslims are terrorists and they should be searched for bombs.'

'Indians cannot be taken seriously, because they are dishonest and they have goofy accents.'

'Coloured people are violent gangsters who are always drunk.'

'All white people are criminals and should be treated as such. We need to take their property, deny them job opportunities and treat them as second-class citizens. White people are rapists, dogs and cowards. We need to sing songs about how they should be mowed down and murdered. According to the white man's religion, women are nothing more than property that can be assaulted and murdered as they please. White people are in the minority and that means that they must have fewer rights than the rest of us ... Absolutely, that is how democracy works. And if they dare to protest against these views, we must tell them to shut their mouths, because they are racists who are simply getting what they deserve.'

Ladies and gentlemen, I do not agree with any single one of the abovementioned quoted statements. I believe them all to be false stereotypes and extremely racist. However, according to the views of the South African government and the ruling ANC, all of the abovementioned statements can be viewed as being racist. All of them, except those relating to white people. In fact, what I have just said regarding white people is a compilation of ANC quotes and policies.

I believe that the topic of whiteness is a misdirected topic. I believe that a solution to the so-called problem of whiteness will do little to move South Africa forward as white people are not to blame for South Africa's contemporary crisis.

I believe that we might just as well initiate a conference about blackness and how black people need to change their way of thinking.

But if we discuss blackness we are only allowed to discuss how black people have been exploited in the past and not how black people need to change their way of thinking. Because the latter would be racist.

If, however, we discuss whiteness we are only allowed to discuss how white people need to change their way of thinking and not how they are currently being exploited. Because the latter would be racist.

That, ladies and gentlemen, is the story of post-apartheid South Africa: a story of double standards. A story in which the President of the country can argue in Parliament that people who are in the minority should have less rights and in which he openly argues that every single thing that is wrong with this country can be laid at the feet of the white man's ancestors.

Now let me state for the record that I do not hold dear my identity as a white man. I believe that the colour of your skin is supposed to be irrelevant. I have also never made a speech about white people, but I am making it now, because that is what I was asked to do. I do, however, regard my religious identity as a Christian as fundamental. I regard my cultural identity as an Afrikaner as an inseparable part of who I am. I regard my geographical identity as an African as non-negotiable.

But am I allowed to be an African? During his famous 'I am an African' speech, former President Thabo Mbeki suggested that I might be. President Jacob Zuma referred to Afrikaners as the white tribe of Africa. I guess in that case, I can be an African.

But according to the laws of this country and the manner in which they are interpreted by our courts, I cannot be an African. The Population Registration Act – a law that was used to categorise people according to the colour of their skin – was repealed because of its racist nature. Ironically, the laws that have been implemented since then continue to discriminate on the basis of race. There is, however, no law according to which different races are categorised. Because to have a law like that would be racist. Furthermore, that is exactly what the ANC fought against. So, what do we do? We scrap the law, but we continue to execute it in any case.

Technically there is no legal basis according to which my race is defined. 'White' is not defined in the Employment Equity Act, nor in the Broad-Based Black Economic Empowerment Act, nor in the Promotion of Equality and Prevention of Unfair Discrimination Act. 'Black', however, is defined as 'a generic term referring to Africans, coloureds and Indians'.

However, 'African' is not defined. According to our Constitution, every citizen has the right to freedom of association and unfair discrimination is prohibited. I associate myself with the term 'African'. Does that mean I am black?

But looking at the way in which the law is applied, it is clear that I cannot be black, simply because I cannot be African, despite my choosing to be referred to as such. I can make a solid argument that this is unfair discrimination and unconstitutional. But that is not how the Constitution is interpreted.

That is why I say that double standards have become the story of South Africa. Let us start with a few examples of the way in which we deal with our history:
- White people are said to be land thieves because they took other people's land. Strange, because that is exactly what Shaka did and it is exactly what Mzilikazi did. Mzilikazi, who committed the greatest genocide in South African history, is however written out of history books and Shaka is rendered a hero. It appears then that where black people killed each other, took each other's land

and even committed genocide, it doesn't matter, because they were black. It seems that #blacklivesmatter, but only when the killers are white. #peopleswar, #ANCvsInkatha, #StompieSeipei.
- The atrocities committed by white people of the Vlakplaas unit of the South African Police (SAP) are stressed in history books. They are held up as an example of white cruelty. At the same time, the tortures of black people committed by the ANC at Quatro and other ANC camps in Africa are ignored.
- We are told that names like Church Street in Pretoria should be changed because offensive names cannot be tolerated. Meanwhile, Amanzimtoti's main street is renamed from Kingsway (hardly offensive) to Andrew Zondo Street. Andrew Zondo, an ANC Youth League member, is really only known for one thing. On 23 December 1985 Zondo planted a bomb in a shopping mall, murdering a baby, a little girl and three women. Some of the families of these murder victims still residing in Amanzimtoti can now drive to work along a street named after the man who murdered their loved ones. But in the South African story of double standards, that is not offensive and the murderer is regarded as a hero, presumably because he was black and because his innocent victims were white.

Now let us look at contemporary examples of double standards:
- When two female students of the University of Pretoria painted themselves black at a private party, they were summarily expelled from their residence before any investigation into the matter could be completed. The South African Students Congress threatened to paralyse universities across the country. The Human Rights Commission (HRC) undertook an investigation into the 'scandal'. Not long afterwards, another photograph was circulated. This time, two white students from the University of Stellenbosch painted their faces black at a fancy dress party. They dressed like Venus and Serena Williams. 'Black face scandal hits Stellenbosch,' one media house reported. As expected, in this case the university also announced that an investigation was being done and the students were forced to publicly apologise for their 'misconduct'.

Before long, the debate became a huge joke on social media. Numerous photographs of black students who painted themselves white or who dressed up like white farmers suddenly surfaced and the general question was why these people were not also being accused of racism. The short answer: because they were black.

- Last year, two white students at the University of the Free State bumped into a black student. The students were accused of having done it deliberately and furthermore of assaulting the black student. It was described as an act of racism. The students were suspended by the university without a hearing, at the insistence of the vice-chancellor, and they were severely insulted in public. However, a court acquitted them of all charges and the HRC found that the incident was not racist. Shortly after this incident almost the same thing happened, but the racial tables were turned, when a white student was thrown from his scooter and assaulted by a black student. The black student was also charged, but in this case the university remained silent in public and the case was soon dropped.
- At the Potchefstroom campus of North West University, the minister of higher education intervened after alleged 'Nazi activities' on campus. An independent inquiry found that there were no Nazi activities on campus, but that did not deter the minister. He stated that he did not care what anyone told him because he was already convinced that the students were busy with Nazi activities. False accusations of Nazism were used as a green light to 'radically transform' the campus, which in practice means that there are too many white people there. Shortly afterwards, a racist pamphlet appeared on campus with the words 'Kill the Boer, Kill the Racist, Kill Afrikaans'. The new vice-chancellor, Professor Dan Kgwadi, said that the university had ordered an investigation into the source of this pamphlet; and then immediately added that the possibility was not being excluded that the pamphlet had actually been distributed by white people.
- When the so-called Rhodes Must Fall campaign was in full swing, the leader of this campaign disrupted classrooms, intimidated white lecturers and stated that white people needed to be killed.

However, this campaign was still regarded as heroic by government and we still hear that its ideals are non-racial.

- When black students at the Elsenburg Agricultural College attacked and assaulted white students with whips, the vice-chancellor and management of the University of Stellenbosch refrained from condemning what had happened. When AfriForum Youth reacted, stating that they would arrange for private security firms to protect innocent students from attacks by rioters, the same university management was said to have replied that AfriForum Youth's response (not the action of rioters who were assaulting people) was polarising the university.
- When white people use the extremely derogatory so-called k-word, a very small group of them argue that the word has a historic meaning that has nothing to do with racism and for that reason the word cannot be regarded as racist; and that how black people feel about the matter is irrelevant. This is a ridiculous argument, of course. But when black people sing about how white people are dogs and rapists and how they should be shot, the very same people who are angered by white people arguing about the k-word, are quick to use the exact same argument to protect these racist songs. They then argue that the song has an historic meaning different from the actual words. They argue that how white people feel about this is irrelevant. The ANC was prepared to go to court to defend their so-called right to sing about murdering white people.

I can continue with more examples, but due to time constraints I shall now conclude.

This phenomenon, ladies and gentlemen, can be called double standards. It can also be labelled black privilege. Black privilege is the privilege to implement racist policies and then call it transformation. Further to that:

- It is the privilege to be able to stand on a stage, in front of the state president, and say that all white people are criminals and should be treated as such, without him blinking an eye.
- It is the privilege to sift potential candidates for appointment as

judges based on their willingness to execute the ANC's political ideology.
- It is the privilege to determine who is legally allowed to be labelled African and who is not.
- It is the privilege to lash out against apartheid for implementing racist policies, but then to turn around and do the exact same thing and get away with it.
- It is the privilege to be admitted to study medicine and become a doctor or a surgeon despite the fact that you did not comply with the minimum requirements for medical school in the first place, while white youths who do comply are turned down because they are white, to make space for you because you are black.
- And worst of all, black privilege is the privilege to believe and argue that your race is so superior that you are excluded from the very definition of racism and that you can never be racist, simply because you are black. That, ladies and gentlemen, is the ultimate form or racism.

I believe that I might have made some people angry with this speech.

If that is the case, I will now do what is expected of white men: I will apologise and I will sit down. But fear not, for this is a democracy. If you want, we can now vote on whether my arguments were valid or not, and you as the majority can outvote me.

But that, I believe, is the new story of South Africa.

The demands of the new world sustain the sins of the old
The parks fable on transformation

XHANTI PAYI

I feel like the way things happened was like everyone sat around the table and talked. Papers were taken from the shelves, put on the table, discussed, divided and signed. And indeed whites agreed to give up this big political office, which had always been closed – doors and windows. And as the whites left in peaceful surrender, with the papers they had taken in the settlement, neatly in a folder and under their arms, in opening the door, let in a gushing wind that had seemed quiet and only a thing of the outside. Left inside, in the political office, is the management of the wind as we collect the papers to put them together without the opportunity ever to close the door, collect the papers, organise them in a way that works. Maybe the door can't be shut.

* * *

The first democratically elected government in South Africa didn't find a bare country. It found a highly developed economy with a strong complement of infrastructure. Even though South Africa was politically and economically isolated in formal terms, it had a highly developed system that embodied many of the values alive in global systems then. Stock exchanges, road networks, wealth accumulation and display, sports teams, musicians and films, and industry. Thus, the most difficult task of the democratic government would not be to manoeuvre international re-inclusion into the global architecture. Challenging as the task of including South Africa back into the international world was, it would be the inclusion of black people – the disenfranchised majority – that would be, and is, still the main and most challenging task. This is the challenge we know as 'transformation'.

South Africa is a well-recognised participant in global economic and geopolitical affairs. It is a job we do with exceptional dexterity. But the shortcomings of the democratic state lie in the democratising of the economy. And this is a result, I would like to argue, of matching the task to overcome the deficiencies and inadequacies bequeathed to the country by the minority government, and the undertakings made to the multitude of interests here at home and abroad. Most challenging is managing and influencing the structures and contours of the open, free and modern economy in attempts to reverse the effects of the old, closed and repressive socio-economic construct. This is to be done in a way in which we all win and endure the least pain.

But there are limited bounties to be shared, beauties to be extended, and deficits and debts to be paid. Are the political values and economic prescripts we have adopted, global as they are, adequate for the work we have to do?

Transformation: Theory and practice

In mathematics, transformation is defined as 'a process by which one figure, expression, or function is converted into another one of similar value' (Oxford Dictionaries, 2015). In English, the Oxford dictionary defines transformation as 'a thorough or dramatic change in form or appearance' (ibid.) Synonyms for transformation in colloquial language might include words such as 'change', 'diversity', 'inclusion', and even terms like 'fair representation'. Indeed, in our own understanding of transformation in South Africa, we have vacillated between the above definitions – in theory and in practice.

In South Africa, social discourse suggests that transformation also represents a measure of the success and meaning of freedom and democracy. How we define transformation, therefore, is central to how we achieve it both in process and conclusion. As we reflect on South Africa since the dawn of democracy, we have to see how far we have come in transforming not just the political sphere, but also the economy.

Essentially, South Africa is trapped in its own attempts to conquer history and form a society that is open within and to the world – accepted in a global market economy. That trap is born from a strategic manoeuvre of and for power, and continues within and outside South African society with its troubled constructs. It is a trap related to what may be a Jean-Jacques Rousseau type of contract, in which the democratic state was formed by a surrender of might and the adoption of law, and by peaceful negotiation into a nation of laws.

Ironically, this trap augurs very dangerously for South Africa as discomfort and tensions rise and threaten the social contract.

In this context, and concentrating on power structures and shifts through the 350 years to 2002, Sampie Terreblanche raises a critical question saying, 'if we take as our point of departure the dismal socio-economic legacy bequeathed to the new government in 1994 by the five racially based periods earlier, the question arises how deep and how comprehensive change towards a new power constellation ought to be before the major problems confronting the new South Africa can be effectively addressed' (Terreblance, 2002: 21).

Terreblanche touches on two critical points relevant to the transformation discussion. The first is the reversal of the legacy of the dismal period prior to 1994; and the second and related point is the power to perform such a reversal within the social contract mentioned above.

By 2002, it was already evident that a new 'power constellation' was necessary, comprising politics and capital, both local and international.

This arrangement remains a critical challenge for the transformation imperative.

Old and new structures

Part of what defines goodness in the new South African society is the bounty and beauty of the leisurely suburbs and urban centres from which black South Africans were excluded. Yes, the roads with pavements, the well-kept parks with wooden chairs, quaint bridges over miniature lakes, charming and shady trees, and lush fields which define this beauty. These features are inviting to all who yearn for a good, picturesque and even healthy lifestyle of afternoon strolls with prams and Saturday morning park runs. But they are not accessible to all.

A new kind of exclusion applies. Where the majority of South Africans were once excluded from this life by law, they are now excluded by financial means. Rising inequality has wrought havoc on the dream of a new South Africa of prosperity and access for all.

These parks, trees and pavements are of such importance in the modern and international society that they lend exclusionary value to surrounding homes.

This means that those who acquired homes in the suburbs before 1994 are reaping the rewards afterwards. The value of these has not only grown since 1994 simply because of parks, but because of what economist Kevin Lings (2014) referred to as the democracy dividend. This can be understood from the perspective that until South Africa was a democratic country it was closed and isolated from the rest of the world. Foreigners could not participate in buying South African assets. They could not bring their dollars to compete for the worth of homes in lush suburbs with parks. As economic theory has shown, competition is an important concept in the determination of value and price. The democracy dividend could thus be said to be the lever that released value compressed in a closed and repressive economic system without competition.

Further, the acceleration of such wealth and the size of the

TOP: *left to right*: Mathews Phosa, Kgalema Motlanthe, Bobby Godsell and Xhanti Payi take stock

BOTTOM: Kgalema Motlanthe and Mary Burton

TOP: The speakers. *Left to right:* Pieter Duvenage, Hein Willemse, Melissa Steyn, Nico Koopman, Mathews Phosa, Mathatha Tsedu, Kgalema Motlanthe, Mary Burton, Xhanthi Payi, Bobby Godsell, Gail Smith, Joel Netshitenzhe

BOTTOM: Kgalema Motlanthe gives his keynote address

OPPOSITE: *top left:* Melissa Steyn, *top right:* Andries Nel, *bottom left:* Mary Burton, *bottom right:* Christi van der Westhuizen

ABOVE AND RIGHT: A captivated audience

OPPOSITE: *top left*: Lynette Steenveld, *top right*: Bobby Godsell, *bottom left*: Dirk Hermann, *bottom right*: Ernst Roets

TOP LEFT: Dirk Hermann, Ernst Roets and Bobby Godsell listen to responses to their inputs

TOP RIGHT: Xhanti Payi

BOTTOM: The audience following closely

OPPOSITE: *top left:* Joel Netshitenzhe stresses a point, *top right:* Mathatha Tsedu, *bottom left:* Pieter Duvenage, *bottom right:* Nico Koopman

TOP: Barry Gilder and Hester du Plessis listen to a contribution from Christi van der Westhuizen

BOTTOM LEFT: Hein Willemse

BOTTOM RIGHT: Mathews Phosa

democratic dividend is a consequence of the initial or low base price of the property or home. First, the land on which the parks are built was easily and cheaply accessible to the minority as a result of the legal regime of exclusion. It was also low because the labour to develop and maintain it was cheaply supplied. Thus, members of white society could accumulate land (property) and its enhancing features and surroundings cheaply. Cheap land, cheap labour and no market forces of competition to pressure value and prices upward kept access open for whites. Relatively poor white people could afford houses then that they could never afford now under an open and competitive economy.

Fast forward to the new and democratic South Africa: all land is open to all to be sold and purchased at competitive market prices. Further, labour is liberated – with oppressive laws repealed and replaced by those supportive of higher labour costs. The rise in labour costs and incomes, an open economy, competitive market prices through the inclusion, not just of the majority of South Africans but of the world, meant soaring land and property prices. So, demand for such land and property escalated, and with it competition and consequently values and prices.

To illustrate the rise in prices and consequent accumulation, the South African Reserve Bank (2015) published statistics on household wealth. The report said household wealth in South Africa had risen by a cumulative 770 per cent to R9.8 trillion since 1994. A significant R2.3 trillion of that wealth is in our homes, while the rest is in financial assets. The parks, freedom and the lure of hope and a rainbow nation are a significant addition in the growth of that wealth and in the context of an open economy. They are enhancements critical to market valuations.

Joseph Stiglitz (2015) makes the argument that it is in fact the ownership and increase in the value of land (urban mainly, although he includes agricultural land more broadly) that has created wealth; and not necessarily the holding of capital as Thomas Piketty has been famed for arguing.

In this respect, Stiglitz supports closely the South African phenomenon of the rise in wealth held in urban land as statistics have shown, as well as rents accumulated from property and land ownership, both urban and agricultural.

Stiglitz further extended his analysis to show that wealth accumulation and distribution have increased as a result of ownership of land, through using it as collateral for loans or credit to access education or start a business. This has no small implication for South Africa, where indeed the booming financial system and markets have been said to keep those without collateral outside and limit their accumulation.

These historic and research perspectives have critical implications for the transformation discussion, and indeed in addressing inequality.

The transformation conundrum

Something important certainly happened in the time since the advent of democracy. Politics succeeded in repealing some of the oppressive structures around labour and allowed the forces of competition to operate in the market. As a result, the incomes of black people have increased markedly, although this bears its debates and limitations.

Data from the 2011 national census released by Statistics South Africa (2012) demonstrates this phenomenon. The income of a black household head increased, on average, by 169 per cent between 2001 and 2011, although it is still only 17 per cent of that of a white household head.

While this can be regarded as a positive thing, the escalation in incomes of the majority has had a cruel twist for the enterprise of transformation.

First, it has increased the cost of constructing and maintaining parks, and thus constrained the government's ability or capacity to expand access to and supply of parks to all neighbourhoods. This means, unlike the case before democracy, the government cannot provide parks that add leisure and value to the neighbourhoods of previously excluded blacks.

Of course, land prices have also kept pace, especially in urban areas. Thus, to attempt inclusion of the black majority in the accumulation, wealth and capital structures under these conditions is proving a challenge, to say the least.

How does transformation happen in these contexts? So restrictive is the rise in wages of the previously exploited that analysts blame this phenomenon for the stalling of economic advance. Thus, it is argued, the South African economy is not growing because it has become globally uncompetitive as wages in the country increase.

Thus, to extend delights and facilitate accumulation for the previously disenfranchised constrains the economy; so do democratic advances and the demands of a modern and global economy. In the same vein, the government may not build low-cost housing alongside the plush suburbs as it may negatively affect the property prices of those who live there. The extension of economic access is in direct contrast to the workings of law and the maintenance of private property.

Long-run wealth and debt patterns

Thomas Piketty and Gabriel Zucman (2015) give us some insight into another phenomenon when they discuss long-run wealth patterns. They show that the aggregate value of wealth in the eighteenth to nineteenth centuries was markedly smaller in the United States than in Europe. Britain and France had a national income double that of the United States at the time the US signed the Declaration of Independence (their social contract) and in the early nineteenth century. This they explain through two phenomena. The first being that there had been no time to save in the new world, the United States; and the second being that the excess supply of land in the new world made it nearly worthless. However, factoring in slavery presents a rather compelling dimension. Because of a shortage of slaves, their value was sky-high in the new world and almost made up for the deficit from land value (in the eyes of owners). However, and critically, Piketty and Zucman note that while this shortage and high value of slaves added to the wealth of slave owners, 'slavery can be viewed as the most extreme form of debt: it should be counted as an asset for the owners and a liability for the slaves, so that net national wealth should be unaffected' (Piketty and Zucman, 2015: 1313–1314). This tells us something critical about economic transformation in South Africa.

South Africa displays some interesting similarities with the relative poverty of the 'new United States' of low savings and slave debt. The majority of black young people in South Africa start on a negative footing since they spend their initial years of work plugging the hole of unearned incomes by their forebears. Even the so-called rising black middle class is constrained by the debt described by Piketty. Because of lack of wealth accumulation by their parents, the black middle class have to pay what is now popularly known as 'the black tax', which includes building their parents decent homes and sustaining both them and themselves while educating and caring for their siblings.

This debt could also be seen even outside the immediate family, in extended family structures and communities. The deficits or loss of income and wealth from apartheid and colonial exploitation of parents or families has to be repaid in this new era. These create further cycles of debt, as historical gaps and deficits take time to close. Reports on savings in South Africa have presented a dismal state of affairs. Gross saving by household continues to be weak, amounting to only 0.1 per cent of gross domestic product (GDP) according to the latest South African Reserve Bank statistics (2016).

In the transformation and inclusion phenomenon, debt has further reach as it has also been part of transformation endeavours in business. Given the denial of black South Africans' participation in the economy and in ownership of assets, black economic empowerment (BEE) has been based on debt structures. Here, blacks or BEE participants have had to borrow to be able to buy shares in big corporates and thus fulfil transformation goals.

This debt trap is especially exacerbated by the vagaries of the free market economy. The borrowing for transformation is done under market conditions, with interest rates and market values determined by open market forces. This means that, unlike in the closed economy period where accumulation was virtually subsidised by government and law, new accumulation is often interrupted and negated by market forces.

To be sure, there has been disquiet also about how the owners of capital (lenders) who used to buy such shares have continued to increase their income, earning interest income through lending into the transformation project.

Structures of debt must thus be recognised as a factor critical to the transformation and indeed reversal of the previous phases before the democratic state of being.

Culture and extensions of capital

The vibrancy of debate that occurs in the media is encouraging, although it is not to be overestimated, and given the status of being representative of all views. Such an interaction happened once between a popular radio presenter and a listener.

The listener, a black male, called into the radio station to complain about the exclusion of talented black players from the national rugby squad. He also felt that this was part of the reason the rugby team had not performed well on a particular occasion. He went on to accuse the coach of racism and racial exclusion, sounding indignant.

The radio presenter, a white male, questioned the reasoning of the caller. In the radio presenter's mind, and expressed to the caller, how could it be that the coach, who obviously wanted to win matches and tournaments, would sabotage himself by excluding evidently talented and worthy players who could contribute to that cause? The presenter rejected the notion entirely as illogical and unreasonable. What the presenter assumed was that the white coach could recognise talent, even if it is not white as he is. What he did not recognise was that the coach could exclude black players on the assumption that including them in the team would actually be the quickest way to lose. This is because the historical periods prior to 1994 created an attitude and culture in white people and against black people. Such an attitude and belief system is now borne out in academic research.

Burns (2009) has examined the impact of racial identity on behaviour in the South African context using experiments with public-high-school students. With participants playing in pairs through strategic proposals, Burns found that non-black players displayed a significantly lower likelihood of strategically engaging with their black partners during the game. Although the experiment is set and played by a selected pool of multi-racial school pupils, it gives us critical insights into social attitudes prevalent in South Africa about blacks. Telzak echoes this finding and observes that negative perceptions about black people were widely held. Telzak refers to interviews he conducted in which a participant stated, 'Black South Africans are lazy. They are complacent. They feel they are entitled. They're dreamers and they're not implementers' (Telzak, 2012: 30–31).

This means that good black players are overlooked for the team; good black bankers are not hired. Thus, the transformation enterprise requires not only a constellation of powers, but of views and attitudes.

A zero-sum game? Conclusions

The goal of transformation is in trouble and there is a desperate need for new initiatives to salvage it. This means that the founding social contract needs revision, requiring implementation of effective interventions constrained by history and legacy, the founding social contract itself, the design of interventions and the structures and contours of the modern economy.

The law and rights environment is blamed for the slow pace of transformation and limitations on redistribution. Rising wages and land prices constrain the repeat of wealth creation as achieved before 1994, while the philosophy and structures of power limit the gains of transformation.

In the modern economy, a rise in the labour share is understood to be in direct conflict with economic growth and the creation of wealth. This is also true for the distribution of wealth, which is discouraged in favour of creation of new wealth or 'baking a bigger pie'.

Economic policy, indeed monetary policy, moves in response to market and global forces. So, the debt defined above must be paid at rates aimed at sustaining the economic system, with limited force in terms of, or toward, internal and historical imperatives. It is difficult to argue with this since the system is what it is.

Terreblanche's question on the need for a constellation of power is critical: 'can empowering the democratically elected government and its bureaucracy be able to play a more active, constructive, and interventionist role in the socio-economic upliftment of the impoverished majority?' (Terreblanche, 2002: 21).

Vito Tanzi (1998) makes an important contribution to the role of government, concluding that 'Inequality is much influenced by systematic factors such as social norms and attitudes, broad economic changes, and governmental activity ... the role of government and the impact of broad economic forces are more important'. He highlights the combined needs of forces that create and defeat inequality asserting, 'Social norms and asset distribution also contribute to the existence of "social capital" and "positional rents" that are very important in maintaining and even creating inequality.'

An important and central question arises as to what sort of policy and interventions may be arranged to effect desired change. What is clear is that the structures of the old world, the pact to secure the new world, and the shortcomings in the constellation of old and new forces are creating tensions and fragilities endangering the entire system. Can the social contract of compromise survive so that there are no losers, and only winners? Again, how does a new constellation of power force change and help the system not to self-destruct?

One thing seems clear: the burdens of debt accumulated through the centuries and exploitation and exclusion are on the shoulders of the free and emerging middle and aspiring capitalist class. The duty to share the bounty and beauty of the country lies upon the state, which, in reality, is increasingly financed by the same middle class.

If these are the causes and demands of the new world, something will have to give, as we see in local protests raising discomfort about the way of the world.

Politicians and economists have to find new ways of being, inserting new and bold ideas into a reimagined constellation of power.

References

Burns, J. (2012) 'Race, diversity and pro-social behaviour in a segmented society'. *Journal of Economic Behaviour and Organisation* 81(2) February 2012: 366–378.

Lings, K. (2014) *The Missing Piece: Solving South Africa's Economic Puzzle*. Johannesburg: Pan Macmillan.

Oxford Dictionaries Language Matters. (2015) *Transformation* available from: http://www.oxforddictionaries.com/definition/english/transformation [accessed January 2016].

Piketty, T. and Zucman, G. (2015) 'Wealth and inheritence in the long run'. Handbook of Income Distribution, Volume 2B: 1303–1368, available at http://piketty.pse.ens.fr/files/PikettyZucman2014HID.pdf

South African Reserve Bank Quarterly Bulletin 277 (September 2015) and 279 (March 2016).

Statistics South Africa. (2012) *Census: 2011*.

Stiglitz, J.E. (2015) 'New theoretical perspectives on the distribution of income and wealth among individuals: part IV land and credit'. *NBER Working Paper* 21192.

Tanzi, V. (1998) 'Fundamental determinants of inequality and the role of government'. *IMF Working Paper* WP/98/178.

Telzak, Samuel C. (2012) 'The tithes of apartheid: perceptions of social mobility among black individuals in Cape Town, South Africa'. *Centre for Social Science Research, University of Cape Town Working Paper* 315.

Terreblanche, Sampie J. (2002) *A History of Inequality in South Africa 1652–2002*. Pietermaritzburg: University of Natal Press.

The World of Ideas
The Place of Afrikaans

The world of ideas
The place of Afrikaans

MATHATHA TSEDU

This session looks at Afrikaans as a language; and we have three very capable people to talk about this. Suffice for me to say that I'm old enough to have done my primary schooling and high schooling under, not Outcomes Based Education (OBE) or any of those fancy things; it was straightforward Bantu Education. It was designed just for me.

So, it didn't include things that I didn't need; and it did exclude things that I really needed to be able to function; and Afrikaans was a very important aspect of the education that I went through. There were a lot of things that we did in Afrikaans like 'Sosialiste ...' I remember doing stuff like 'redes vir die hervorming, die Pope is as onfeilbaar beskou'. All of that was drummed into me and when I got to matric, I realised that even if I passed all the other subjects with flying colours, if I failed Afrikaans I was not going to get my certificate.

So, it was an important language which I had to pass, and it was also, of course, an instrument of oppression. Whether you were going to the post office or anywhere, the police station, that was the language that was used there, and it was used with a lot of arrogance and it's the kind of arrogance that you still find today, really, among many people who speak Afrikaans who are white.

I get my pay from Media 24. I work at the South African National Editors Forum. I'm seconded by Media 24. So, I must be careful what I say about Media 24 because Adriaan is here. He might want to argue for an increase through me. When I was hired at Media 24 I was to edit *City Press*, which is an English publication. But one of the questions that I had to deal with was whether I was fluent in Afrikaans. So, I said, 'well I got a C in matric, you know'. Meetings were generally held in Afrikaans. I remember Khatu Mamaila, who was also working with me, going to one of these meetings and the people kept yap-yapping in Afrikaans and when it was his turn to speak he spoke in Venda and there was a big silence in the room. Khatu said, 'Well if you are going to continue like that then English is also not my language but I've done my 50 per cent. So, if you are not even going to do yours I'll stand here and you stand there and let's see how far we get.'

Recently I've gone into a bit of farming up in Limpopo and there's a farmers' meeting. (You know, I'm a farmer, so if people start singing kill this or that sometimes I say okay.) So, you go to these meetings because they are important. You are discussing the ticks that are now in vogue with the cattle and all sorts of very important stuff and people just continue in Afrikaans. They just assume you understand. I have a guy who works with me on the farm who is from Zimbabwe. But sometimes I send him to the meetings and he comes back and he can't tell me what happened, but it is just assumed that you must understand. There isn't even any attempt at moving a bit. So, it's the arrogance that I'm talking about that one finds around the language as an instrument that is still being used.

When I was at *City Press* we ran a bursary called the Percy Qoboza Bursary, a portion of which was attainable at Rhodes (which must fall) and another portion was at Stellenbosch (which must open up). We were taking students through the journalism department and they were doing it in English and then a decision was taken within the company that, because somebody much, much higher up within Naspers thinks that Stellenbosch must actually remain an Afrikaans-medium institution it is contradictory for the company to continue to send people who are going to learn in English at an institution that this person who is quite important in the company feels shouldn't be doing all this English stuff. So, the bursary was cancelled and we took the money and moved it to Tshwane University of Technology. I'm saying all this to try to say that language is very important and Afrikaans, in particular, is still being used to sustain a legacy that shouldn't be here with us today. And, for me, I was sad to hear Dirk and Ernst here. I was angry, ja. I was angry.

I was angry that you come into a place like this, which is a place of serious pain, and say such things. I passed through here as a detainee. I left a little girl here who was being detained. We were moving to Morningside police station and we were being driven to Groenpunt in the Free State but she was going to remain here. We dropped her here. The next time I heard about her was when one prisoner had smuggled a piece of newspaper into the prison in Groenpunt and I read it and she had died of complications with her headaches. When we were with her at Morningside she had been brought there after a month of torture maybe in Vlakplaas or somewhere. She had been tortured horribly. She was asthmatic. They had taken away all her medication. They brought her here and when she was released she lasted a month and she died. So, this is a place of pain. A pain that was inflicted through this language that we are now going to be dealing with here today.

Afrikaner intellectual history
An interpretation

PIETER DUVENAGE

It is a daunting task to interpret Afrikaner intellectual history.[1] How can one provide a representative picture of a diverse and complex group of people with an equally complicated history? A people that have been heavily criticised and blamed in recent times, but also throughout their history.[2] This paper must be seen as *an* interpretation and not *the* interpretation of Afrikaner intellectual history.[3] For this reason, it is presented in the spirit of both dialogue and critical debate

---

[1] This paper was originally published in P. Vale, L. Hamilton and E. Prinsloo (eds). (2014). *Intellectual Traditions in South Africa. Ideas, Individuals and Institutions.* Pietermaritzburg: University of KwaZulu-Natal Press: 73–94. The author gratefully thanks the publisher for permission to reuse the paper here.
[2] See in this regard Dan O'Meara. (1996). *Forty Lost Years: The Apartheid State and the Politics of the National Party, 1948–1994.* Johannesburg: Ravan Press.
[3] A. du Toit and H. Giliomee (1983) still remain authoritative on the topic. For a more conventional version see G.D. Scholtz (1967–1979), and for an overview F.A. van Jaarsveld (1981): 1–72. I want to thank Johann Rossouw and Peter Vale for their critical inputs during the writing of this contribution.

– not just among Afrikaners, but also between Afrikaners and other South Africans, and beyond the country's borders, too.

Who are Afrikaners? Where do they come from? And how have they understood themselves throughout 350 years of South African history? In what follows, these three questions will be answered in a brief and fairly standard manner. In order to do so, however, I offer a historical reconstruction of the main phases of Afrikaner political thought. This begins by looking at its earliest origins and takes the story up to 1795, when the English took over from the Dutch as colonial masters of the Cape. The next phase (1795–1910) is one of reaction against British imperialism. It offers answers in the form of the republican state idea in the north and, in the Cape Colony, multi-party accommodation. Third, there was the era of unitary and exclusionary state building which ran from 1910 to 1994 – that is, the duration of both the Union and the Republic until the ending of formal apartheid. This political-historical reconstruction is interconnected with cultural-intellectual movements in religion, in politics and in education – all of which have shaped Afrikaner intellectual life. Finally, the intellectual position of Afrikaners after the loss of state power in 1994 is considered: here, the focus falls on recent positions taken by Afrikaner intellectuals. These include N.P. van Wyk Louw (1906–1970) on liberal nationalism; Johan Degenaar (born 1926), whose work can be read as a pluralist logic allowing for individual, group and class differences, without losing sight of mutual commitment; Hermann Giliomee (born 1938) on political pluralism; and Danie Goosen (born 1953) on minorities in South Africa. The early choice of the concept *interpretation* to describe this paper is also not without reason. It is influenced by Hans-Georg Gadamer's notion of philosophical hermeneutics – being a philosopher of interpretation with a strong historical sense. On this occasion, space does not permit an exhaustive discussion of Gadamer's work, but his ideas, coupled with Isaiah Berlin's distinction between negative and positive liberty, Michael Sandel's communitarian concepts of the unencumbered and encumbered selves, and the distinction between a unitary or federal form of politics, form the central theoretical underpinnings of the argument.

Gadamer's major book, *Truth and Method,* consists of three parts. In the first, aesthetical, part the experience of the artwork is not exclusively determined by the subject because the subject can undergo change in the experience of the artwork. This ontological conception of aesthetics also works through to Gadamer's conception of history and tradition (part II of *Truth and Method*) as well as his conception of language as the medium of hermeneutical experience (part III of *Truth and Method*).[4] As in the case of the perception of art, language is not grounded exclusively in the consciousness of the individual subject, but mainly in the language that we call dialogue or conversation. In a similar fashion, the consciousness of every person is influenced by history; and that consciousness stands open to the effects or the working of history as play, the so-called working-historical consciousness (*wirkungsgeschichtliches Bewusstsein*) (Gadamer, 1960: 285/2004: 301). In short, one's understanding (consciousness) of oneself in the world is always historical, linguistic and contingent (Wright, 1998). This brings us to two other historically relevant concepts of Gadamer: the *hermeneutical circle* – in which the whole is understood through the parts and the parts through the whole – and the *fusion of horizons*. Such a fusion takes place where the horizon of an artwork, historical text or other culture is brought into critical dialogue with the horizon of the interpreter. In this case the horizon of Afrikaner intellectual history will be brought into a critical dialogue with the horizon of the interpreter speaking here. In the hermeneutical situation, an interpreter is primarily engaged with the tradition he or she is trying to understand.[5]

Given that these concepts of interpretation and understanding will

---

[4] Similar to aesthetic experience (of an art object like a painting or novel) the act of understanding is not merely a cognitive-subjective act, but a working historical consciousness. It is more about being than consciousness – *meer syn as bewus*syn (Warnke, 1987: 79–80; Schoeman, 1983: 15–16). On aesthetical play, see H-G. Gadamer, (1960: 97/2004: 103).

[5] On situation, see H-G. Gadamer (1960: 285/2004: 301), on horizon (1960: 286/2004: 301) and the fusion of horizons (1960: 290/2004: 305). Gadamer's concept of application, which is linked with the above-mentioned concepts, owes a lot to Aristotle's (2009: Book VI) concept of *phronesis*. For a full explanation, see Duvenage (2013).

inform this paper, it should be clear that it is written from a specific perspective – or horizon, as Gadamer puts it. It is not, therefore, a neutral academic exercise; it is, instead, an interpretation of the intellectual history of a specific community from the inside-out. The danger, of course, is that this approach can easily be seen as too subjective. Nevertheless, my hope is to share and communicate these issues as universally as possible. Both my own, and recipients', epistemological challenge can be read in the answers to two questions: How can the intimate-particular be communicated universally? What is the relationship between subjective experience and universal reflective knowledge?

Origins

For all its local character, the history of Afrikaners begins in the drama that unfolded between Jerusalem and Athens/Rome: the Judeo-Christian world on the one hand and the worlds of Athens/Rome on the other. But the essential features of the Afrikaner intellectual tradition were forged in Europe in the long march through the Middle Ages, the Renaissance, the Reformation and early modernity, especially the nascent state system of the seventeenth century. In the form of the Dutch they landed as part of European modernising expansion – itself driven by the age of discovery – at the southern tip of Africa as employees of one of the first multinational corporations in world history.

Given these conditions, it is easy to understand why it was that Jan van Riebeeck (and his party) did not bring a library of books with them to the Cape of Good Hope when they landed in 1652. Van Riebeeck's instructions were more practical than conceptual: he was tasked to establish a commercial settlement, at a place located halfway between the Netherlands and Java, in order to provide fresh produce to East Indiamen plying one of the most profitable sea routes in the world. In these circumstances, there was much to be done and little time to luxuriate in intellectual and philosophical reflection. The Dutch East India Company (VOC), which founded the settlement that would become South Africa, had little interest in the hinterland: reports declared this as barren, inhospitable, and populated by 'primitive' peoples. Such interests as there may well have been waned when exploring parties failed to find any workable mineral deposits. For a century and a half, the VOC governed the Cape according to a central idea: profit. This (and the idea that Holland was home) discouraged the spread of settlement much beyond what today we call the Hottentots-Holland Mountains (Coetzee, 1988: 1). Even though some rudimentary institutions normally associated with intellectual life were founded, it was difficult to bring about the life of the mind. O.F. Mentzel, for example, wrote almost a hundred years after Van Riebeeck's arrival that: '[t]here are no high schools or universities in this country. Such institutions are not required, for what use could one make of learning acquired there in a land where life is still primitive and where the Company's rule is law' (Mentzel, 1919: 108–109 in Schoeman 1997: 54). Within the closed culture of the VOC, the Dutch at the Cape were initially certainly colonists bounded by a regime of profit and loss. But when they became free burghers (*vryburgers*) and began to call themselves Afrikaners, a qualitatively different relationship started to develop between them and the land: the colonial company was no longer their beginning and their end.[6] From that moment, a tension started to develop between their European past and their African future. They became a people caught between Europe and Africa. It is quite understandable that their first encounters with the indigenous population (first the Khoisan and later the black groups on the eastern border and, still later, further inland) would lead to misrecognition and conflict.[7] Anthony Holiday (1993: 5) puts it aptly: 'For better or worse, the theoretical reaches

---

[6] This is illustrated by the first noted case of a Dutch settler in the Cape Colony publicly calling himself an Afrikaner. I refer here to Hendrik Biebouw, who declared in the early 1700s, after being arrested for rowdy public behaviour in Stellenbosch, '*Ik ben een Afrikaander*' (see Giliomee, 2004: 40).

[7] On first contact situations, see Diamond (2005): 205–206; and for an historical and systematic reflection on recognition and misrecognition, see Honneth (1995).

of our life-forms have a capacity to shape our attitudes towards ourselves and the inhabitants of other cultural settings, which is every bit as potent as the determinations effected by religio-ethical, poetic or artistic dimensions of the cultural habitat.'

In southern Africa, where so many different social groups encountered each other in a harsh, though beautiful, country, conflict was to be expected: these were not only between white and black, but also between black groups and between black and Khoisan peoples. In such a cauldron of misrecognition, unmediated prejudice and unequal relationships, Afrikaners-in-the-making used technological resources as well as European ideas and political institutions to their considerable advantage.

Despite Mentzel's reservations, a greater cultural and political self-consciousness developed in the second half of the eighteenth century among Afrikaners and they began to reflect on their lived experience. This deepening self-consciousness was the result of a mix of material and intellectual developments. Important among them were the institutionalisation of Dutch Calvinism, the building of towns in the near interior and the development of a specific – and skewed – system of economic exchange. These were supported by a rudimentary educational system and they gave increasing legitimacy to an emergent government system that drew on administrative principles and political ideas in the public domain. This resulted in a deepening sense of self-reliance – first against the VOC, and, when the British successively occupied the Cape, their colonial authority and institutions. This expanding self-consciousness, though, had a distinct downside: a strong racial consciousness developed among Afrikaners in the Cape by the mid-eighteenth century. They saw themselves as both white and Christian – qualities they considered to be both different and superior to other racial groups living in the Cape. In this habitus (to use Bourdieu's term), the ideas of race and class became increasingly associated with each other and this explains why, as Afrikaner farmers moved into the interior, the question of land ownership became a burning issue. As Giliomee (1975: 22) puts it, by the end of the eighteenth century, white prejudice was strongly entrenched in Cape Town, as well as in the interior from the eastern border to what is today called Colesberg and further northwards. Whites, mostly Afrikaners, formed a governing class that excluded others, both economically and politically. Against this background, Afrikaner self-consciousness and group formation showed both a positive and a negative side. It brought to the fore a degree of self-reliance and self-consciousness as opposed to a distant and alien governance system first of the VOC and, later, of British colonialism. But it operated in an exclusionary manner – group privilege (and superiority) determined this, especially when it came to the Other.

Notwithstanding the passage of history, this remains the basic dilemma of Afrikaners in South Africa. Where group formation always occurs on the basis of 'we' against 'they', the quandary is that initial Afrikaner group formation took place vis-à-vis a distant white colonial, higher class 'them' *and* a proximate non-white indigenous, lower class 'them'.[8] This dualism made for an ambiguous form of group identity that has manifested itself in a moral – say, anti-colonial – form, *as well as* an immoral racist form. The resulting tension is internal to Afrikaner identity as it has unfolded historically, making for the most attractive as well as the most unattractive moments – indeed, decades – in the country's history.

The search for self-expression

By the time the British first occupied the Cape (1795), some constituent elements of group identity were in place among Afrikaners: a specific language (in the form of an increasingly indigenised Dutch called Afrikaans); a single church group in the Dutch Reformed tradition but with many different internal traditions; a colour consciousness that has already been discussed; and, finally, general societal alignment with Dutch – as opposed to British – intellectual and political traditions. But, importantly, other features necessary for the

---

[8] This dialectic was undoubtedly intensified through the Afrikaner experience of slave ownership. The historians Hermann Giliomee (2004): 55–56 and Karel Schoeman (2013) – to name but two – have done important work on the theme.

development of a national consciousness were absent – for example, the theological and educational tradition was fragmentary; there were no real intellectual leaders and (borrowing from Benedict Anderson's 1983 insights) there was no independent press. As Giliomee (1975: 26–27) put it, there was a feeling of *lotsverbondenheid* (mutual fate), but a *volksgevoel* (national feeling) was still to develop.

After 1806, and the second and final occupation of the Cape by Britain, Afrikaner self-consciousness – and, with this, their intellectual history – entered new terrain. This phase was one in which the distant white, colonial, higher class – a 'them' rather than an 'us' – became both proximate and threatening. This was especially so from 1820 as the British embarked on robust anglicisation of local political and bureaucratic institutions. So, English became the language of the civil service, the courts and (after its establishment) the Cape Parliament (Giliomee, 1975: 27). This *verengelsing* (anglicisation) also took place in education as increasingly this was institutionalised through state funding. In addition, the country's early institutions of higher education – the South African College, now the University of Cape Town (1829), St Andrew's College, now Rhodes University (1855), Grey College, now the University of the Free State (1855), and Victoria College, now the University of Stellenbosch (1874) – were strongly influenced by both British intellectual and administrative traditions.

It was against the potential material benefits which flowed from this that a split developed among Afrikaners in the Cape Colony. By the late 1830s, a considerable number of people who called themselves Afrikaners decided to quit British authority – most of these were located on the Colony's north-eastern border. Their compatriots remained in the Cape as loyal British subjects for most of the nineteenth century without surrendering their church, or their Dutch-Afrikaans language – the two pillars of a culture-in-the-making. The Afrikaners who moved beyond the borders of the Cape were the heirs of a long-festering resentment against British rule. The first stirrings of this search for independence – the so-called Patriot movement of the late-1770s (which was against the Dutch authorities) – became ever stronger during the British colonisation of the Cape and contributed to near-systematic northern movement of people, known as the Great Trek. It was especially the experience of alienation, of being a colonised colonist, that contributed to a strong yearning for collective and individual liberty. This must be seen as a version of positive liberty or positive freedom rather than negative liberty – to use a well-known distinction made by Isaiah Berlin (1984: 15–36) and further developed by Michael Sandel (1982, 1984, 2009).

Negative liberty means freedom from external interference (Berlin, 1984: 19), which Sandel (1984: 4–5) calls the unencumbered self. The notion is essentially about maximum freedom – especially the maximum freedom of the individual to be divorced from his or her surroundings. It is an understanding of freedom that many Afrikaners today, like people elsewhere, follow (this will be elaborated on later). For Berlin, positive freedom is the freedom to live a specific life – or being able to live a free life. Berlin (1984: 22) writes, 'For the "positive" sense of liberty comes to light if we try to answer the question, not "What am I free to do or be?", but "By whom am I ruled?"'or "Who is to say what I am, and what I am not, to be or do?" The connection between democracy and individual liberty is a good deal more tenuous than it seemed to many advocates of both.' Similar ideas were earlier explored in the writing of T.H. Green in *The Principles of Political Obligations* (1886) and of Bernard Bosanquet in *The Philosophical Theory of the State* (1899): interestingly, both these books were published during the time of the ZAR and the Free State Republic. For Green, the neo-Hegelian concept of freedom is one where 'the whole of man' finds its goal.

While Berlin eventually chooses negative liberty over positive liberty in his inaugural lecture of 1958, Michael Sandel offered a different take on these two notions in the 1980s. Recalling Hegel's arguments against Kant, Sandel (1984: 5) connects positive liberty to communitarian critics of modern (rights-based) liberalism who 'question the claim for the priority of the right over the good, and the picture of the freely-choosing individual it embodies. Following Aristotle, they argue that we cannot justify political arrangements without references to common purposes and ends, and that we cannot conceive of our personhood without reference to our role as citizens, and participants in a common life.' Here Sandel refers to a situated, narrative and encumbered self: 'I am situated from the start, embedded in a history which locates me among others, and implicates my good in the good of the communities whose stories I share' (1984: 9). Similar to Gadamer's concept of the hermeneutical self in his philosophical hermeneutics, at issue here is not a personal self in isolation, but one dialogically linked with others – and all influenced by a common good rather than abstract rights. One could argue that the Afrikaners of the Patriot movement (in the eighteenth century), the Voortrekkers and the Burghers of the Orange Free State and the ZAR (in the nineteenth century) lived according to the concept of positive freedom – an encumbered, situated and hermeneutical self – as was later theorised by Berlin and Sandel. But what happened to the Afrikaners who remained in the Cape Colony at that time? Did they work with what we now call a positive or negative concept of liberty, an encumbered or unencumbered version of the self?

In the interior of the country, the Voortrekkers succeeded in forming a number of states that stood in a federal-independent relation with the Cape Colony (as part of the British Empire) and the native population. As an example of the less salient aspects of Afrikaner identity formation vis-à-vis the indigenous 'them', it is important to note that both Voortrekker-Boer states in the nineteenth century did not include the native population in the state, while the Cape Colony had from the middle of the century a qualified franchise. From their very beginning, the Voortrekkers were republicans, but also in terms of their sense of belonging they were decidedly federalists and non-secular republicans. It seems ironic that it was these federal-republicans who would lay the foundations for the unitary state that was established in 1910. Why? If the Voortrekkers had lost the 1839 encounter, which is known by the descendants of the Voortrekkers as the Battle of Blood River, chances are good that the whole Trekker movement would have been halted. Had this happened, South Africa's history as a unitary state would have turned out differently. The outcome at Blood River decisively contributed to the creation of different Trekker states in the nineteenth century according to the political philosophy of federal-republicanism. It was the creation of the Republiek van die Oranje-Vrystaat (Free State Republic) and the

ZAR – as widely recognised states which pursued republican ideals and followed cultural norms – that eventually clashed with the British imperialist goals for southern Africa leading to the war of 1899–1902, which today is called the South African War but has also been called the Boer War and the Anglo-Boer War. The unitary state that was established on 31 May 1910 and is now called South Africa was established in its aftermath.

Before discussing the Union of South Africa, which is what this state was called, we must briefly reconstruct the institutionalisation of Afrikaner intellectual life from the middle of the nineteenth century to the early twentieth century. In an article in 1947, the philosopher A.H. Murray (1909–1995) showed how church and theological debates contributed to Afrikaner intellectual (and philosophical) history. Afrikaners, he writes 'have appropriated their experience and theories about local government rather from their experience with church governance (*kerklike bestuur*) than from the example of civil governance that came from the Castle and its environment' (Murray, 1947: 168). This reveals an intimate relation between the Church and politics that was strengthened by the emergence of two (essentially northern) versions of the Dutch Reformed Church in the south: the Nederduitsch Hervormde Kerk (formed in 1854); and the Gereformeerde Kerk (formed in 1859). Although these were similar to their mother institution, the Cape-centred Dutch Reformed Church (Nederduitse Gereformeerde Kerk), small but eventually decisive theological differences emerged as they broke away to form their own synods.

The first important indigenous theological debate within the Cape Dutch Reformed Church took place at the General Synod of 1862. The heart of the matter was an orthodox (or literal) interpretation of the Bible as against a more historical-critical interpretation that used more modern and rationalist rules of interpretation – the so-called liberal interpretation. The latter was supported by figures like J.J. Kotze (1832–1902) and T.F. Burgers (1834–1881), who were influenced by the Utrecht School of Opzoomer, Scholten and Kuenen (Murray, 1947: 170). Drawing from the ideas of thinkers like Auguste Comte and J.S. Mill, they were criticised for applying the methodology of natural science to the terrains of psychology, theology and philosophy. Lined up against them were more orthodox figures like G.W.A. van der Lingen (1804–1869), N.J. Hofmeyr (1827–1909), John N. Murray (1826–1882), and his brother Andrew Murray (1828–1917), who linked the religious experience to the transcendent.[9] Although the conservatives emerged victorious, the various views were long debated in a slowly evolving public sphere both in the Cape and elsewhere in the country. Letters, articles and comments were published in the emerging Dutch/Afrikaans press – especially in *De Zuid Afrikaan* (first published in 1830) and the liberal *De Onderzoeker*. It soon became clear, to clergy and lay-person alike, that the debate was much wider than its narrow theological setting. It touched on the relation between religion and the transcendent; the application and limits of scientific method to scriptural interpretation; the difference between belief and critical scrutiny; and the relationship between Church and State. According to Murray (1947: 173), 'the liberal struggle of 1862 ... strengthened a spiritual rather than a naturalistic outlook [*lewensuitkyk*] among the people [*volk*]'.[10] Unsurprisingly, these issues resurfaced in many subsequent theological debates among Afrikaners: for example, in the famous Stellenbosch case around the alleged liberal theology of Professor Johannes du Plessis (1868–1935) in the 1920s and 1930s. The liberal-orthodox divide in Afrikaner theological debates, which remains until today, emphasises the importance of dealing systematically and logically with the issue of values as well as underscoring the need for a certain sensitivity over the fact that concrete actions – practice – are always dialectically related to principles – theory.

This particular outlook also found fertile ground in the emerging educational debate among Afrikaners at Dutch-Afrikaans institutions of higher education in places such as Stellenbosch and Burgersdorp, and northwards in Bloemfontein, Pretoria and Potchefstroom. Aside from the theological-centred debates, questions were raised

---

[9] On Hofmeyr, see Kestell (1911).
[10] My translation of: '[die] liberale stryd van 1862 ... [het] 'n geestelike in teenstelling met 'n naturalistiese in die lewensuitkyk van die volk ... versterk.'

in these places that could not simply remain on a practical level. Questions like these: What is knowledge? What is a human and, more specifically, what is a child? Is there a place for religion in education? Afrikaner educationists in this period reacted against two influential educational trends in the British Empire – namely naturalism (which drew on Darwin's theory of evolution) and a kind of psychologism that worked with naturalist categories. Their answers to these ideas were a milder Christian-phenomenological education or a stricter Calvinist version of man and society (Murray, 1947: 178–179).

These kinds of debate did not leave the political and constitutional terrain untouched. A number of far-reaching debates followed on the principles of Roman-Dutch law; the contribution of the Dutch Reformed churches to civil governance; the struggle about the freedom of the press in the 1820s and 1830s; the Trek manifestos; and the constitutional arrangements in the South African and Free State republics. All these ideas on theology, education and politics were characterised by a strong sense of anti-naturalism and were carried on into the twentieth century (Murray, 1947: 187).

The last terrain that contributed to the self-awakening of Afrikaners was the language movement, first through the Genootskap vir Regte Afrikaners (Association of True Afrikaners) that emerged in Paarl in 1875 and in which the Reverend S.J. du Toit (1847–1911) played a leading role.[11] Although it started in the Cape, it had religious and ethnic-political undercurrents that were felt right across the country and across two centuries. One of the underlying impulses for the formation of a language movement was to unite all Afrikaners on the basis of a common language and an emerging culture. An increasingly exclusive concept of Afrikaners functioned in opposition to the reconciliatory politics of J.H. (Onze Jan) Hofmeyr (1845–1909), leader of the Cape Afrikaners, who had a more inclusive concept of Afrikaners, which included both coloured speakers of the language and speakers of English in his Cape-centred Afrikanerbond party at the end of the nineteenth century (see Davenport, 1966).

---

[11] For a recent sympathetic biography, see D'Assonville (1999).

The exclusionary state

How did Afrikaners see themselves in the South African state after 1910? The answer to this question must be set against both their intellectual tradition of positive freedom, encumbered-hermeneutical selves, their preference for a federal South Africa, and the history of their cultural-political institutionalisation (religion, education, political arrangements and language struggle).

Northern-based Afrikaners were forced to come to terms with the devastation of the South African War and the complete disappearance of their political and symbolic order. They also found themselves in the midst of what today would be called 'deeply structural change'. The economic transformation of South Africa was under way and driven by mining and industrialisation, and this contributed to the rapid urbanisation of all South Africans, including Afrikaners. The movement of Afrikaners to the city as reported by Giliomee (1975: 35) is as follows: 10 per cent (1900) to 41 per cent (1926), 50 per cent (1936) and 75 per cent (1960). As a result the socio-economic circumstances of Afrikaners changed completely: in the late-1800s they had been a relatively self-sustaining agrarian people; thirty years later a quarter of them were classified as 'poor-whites' by the Carnegie Report and the others were far from well off. In the rapidly growing cities they had to compete with blacks and English capital, in institutions that were largely unaccommodating (Giliomee, 1975: 36).

The question that faced Afrikaners was this: How should their self-consciousness and collective identity continue in the new state? In order to answer this question it is important to look at the formation of South Africa as a unitary state in 1910, one of ambiguity. On the one hand it included whites, blacks, coloureds and Indians, but with voting rights only for the two white groups – only in the newly proclaimed Cape 'Province' was there a highly qualified franchise for coloureds and blacks. The question whether South Africa would become more of a segregated or integrated country was left to future generations. The reconciliation between Afrikaners and English speakers was uneasy. Memories of the Boer War, especially the deaths of thousands of women and children in concentration camps, were still fresh, and Afrikaners felt that their language, culture, history and religion were threatened (Giliomee, 1975: 36). Despite the attempts by two Boer War generals – Louis Botha (1862–1919) and the Cambridge-trained Jan Smuts (1874–1950) – to reconcile the two groups (through the South African Party), they were soon opposed by another Boer War general, J.B.M. (Barry) Hertzog (1866–1942), who was the main force behind the foundation of the National Party (NP) in 1914. Hertzog's position was strengthened by the growth of cultural movements within Afrikaner civil society. Die Suid-Afrikaanse Akademie vir Wetenskap en Kuns (South African Academy for Science and Art) was formed in 1909. The second language movement promoted Afrikaans above what was called High Dutch and sought to foster a literature by authors such as Jan F.E. Celliers (1865–1940), C. Louis Leipoldt (1880–1947), Totius (1877–1953); and to ensure, through the work of C.J. Langenhoven (1873–1932), that Afrikaans received an equal place to English in both state structures and education (Wessels, 2010). Other Afrikaner-centred institutions were the secretive and exclusionary Afrikaner Broederbond (Afrikaner Brotherhood, 1918); the Federasie vir Afrikaanse Kultuurverenigings (FAK Federation for Afrikaans Cultural Societies, 1929), a sort of umbrella body for all Afrikaner cultural societies, and the Reddingsdaadbond (Rescuing Union); to unite all Afrikaner businesses in a cultural-communitarian movement with strong social democratic and even socialist undertones.

The crucial question, though, is what became of the Afrikaners' encumbered-hermeneutic concept of the self and republican-federalist political philosophy as explained earlier regarding the cultural-political institutionalisation of the nineteenth century. What kind of reasoning convinced Afrikaners, especially northerners, against their political instincts to accept a unitary South Africa in 1910? Three possible answers can be offered here. The first was pragmatic: the price of remaining within the Western sphere of influence was acceptance of the British Empire. Second, the formation of the four provinces, based on the Canadian model, provided for contractual relationships between centre and periphery. Finally, Afrikaners as the voting majority in the new state could – certainly theoretically and indeed practically – control their own fate if linked to the idea of positive freedom. The Afrikaner co-founders of a unitary South Africa – whether they were Botha/Smuts on the one hand or Hertzog and the former president M.T. Steyn (1857–1916) on the other – thought about South Africanness not with the liberal notion of individuality, but in accordance with the idea of positive liberty or encumberedness. South Africa, in this view, was a nation of groups, not mere individuals. This perspective offered a double bind that would haunt Afrikaner thinking: though the immediate division was based on language, this hid a more ominous divide: race; and, second, the management of the divide was to be centrally steered by the state in the twentieth century.

By the early 1930s Hertzog, prime minister from 1924 to 1939, felt that the time was ripe for Afrikaners and English speakers to become one nation, and together with Smuts he formed the United Party. Ranked against them was the Purified National Party (Gesuiwerde Nasionale Party) of D.F. Malan (1874–1959), who had taken his doctorate at Utrecht. For Malan, English-speaking South Africans still considered England as their home and, infinitely more importantly, he believed that Afrikaners should return the country to their republican roots. Malan's political understanding was also linked to the poor white issue and the need for Afrikaners to make material progress in a country dominated by English business interests. But Malan's political position rested on an ethnic-communitarian argument that Afrikaners had the democratic right to lead South Africa towards a republic. In this he was assisted by a younger brand of modernising nationalist politicians – Eric Louw (1890–1968), C.R. Swart (1894–1982), J.G. Strijdom (1893–1958), Eben Dönges (1898–1968), Paul Sauer (1899–1976) and H.F. Verwoerd (1901–1966). Strong support was also forthcoming from Afrikaner civil society which was, as we have seen, quite developed; as well as the three Dutch Reformed churches, academics at the increasingly confident universities in Stellenbosch, Bloemfontein, Potchefstroom and Pretoria, writers and poets whose work was well known, as well as the business community. This more democratic version of Afrikaner nationalism was strongly challenged by a more militant and radical form of authoritarian nationalism during World War II – the Ossewabrandwag (Oxwagon Sentinel) led by an able orator, Hans van Rensburg (1898–1968), and intellectuals such as Piet Meyer (1909–1982). With the demise of Germany in the Second World War the influence of the Ossewabrandwag also dwindled, but certain of its members found a way back to the NP.

Although narrow, the 1948 victory of the NP meant that Afrikaners, without the help of the English speakers, had succeeded in taking power in a unitary state. Their immediate projects were the establishment of a republic in 1961 and the implementation of the apartheid policy, which Hendrik Verwoerd later called 'separate development'.[12] Both of these can be seen against the background of positive freedom as developed by Sandel in communitarian terms – inasmuch as Afrikaners strove to establish an independent state where they could pursue their collective freedom as a community and notwithstanding the historical ambiguity of this community's identity. The problem, though, was that the NP, strengthened by the technocratic and instrumental power of the modern state it inherited; further entrenched racial divisions; which can be understood as an unattractive example of the part of Afrikaner identity that constituted itself in opposition to the non-white, lower-class indigenous 'them'. This was a twisted version of the communitarian-hermeneutic self where a minority group tried, with all the state power at its disposal, to force a twisted federalism, consisting of white South Africa and the bantustans, onto the majority. If it had succeeded it would have meant the end of South Africa as a unitary state. Until his assassination in 1966, Verwoerd thought about South Africa (and the protectorates Swaziland, Lesotho and Botswana) as a commonwealth of states. After Verwoerd the NP, under internal and external pressure,

---

[12] At the beginning of his career as minister, Verwoerd described the scope of apartheid in the following terms, as quoted in Davenport (1977): 270: 'Apartheid comprises a whole multiplicity of phenomena. It comprises the political sphere; it is necessary in the social sphere; it is aimed at in church matters; it is relevant to every sphere of life. Even within the economic sphere it is not just a question of numbers. What is of more importance there is whether one maintains the colour bar or not.'

reluctantly returned to the idea of South Africa as unitary state by the mid-1980s.[13]

It must also be added that the policy of apartheid was never without powerful critics – both externally and from within. While the external opponents and critics are well known, it is often forgotten that there was also a minority of powerful critics, from early on, among Afrikaners: theologians such as Bennie Keet (1885–1974), Ben Marais (1909–1999) and Beyers Naudé (1915–2004). There were also Afrikaner figures in opposition politics such as Henry Fagan (1889–1963), Japie Basson (1918–2012) and Frederik van Zyl Slabbert (1940–2010); literary figures such as Jan Rabie (1920–2001) and the whole literary Sestiger-beweging of André P. Brink (1935–2015), Breyten Breytenbach (born 1939) and others; and so-called verligte (enlightened) journalists such as Piet Cillie (1917–1999) and Schalk Pienaar (1916–1978). The remarkable thing is that, by the mid-1980s, leading Afrikaner politicians, intellectuals, artists (for example, the youth revolt of the so-called Voëlvry rock music movement) and business people had turned their backs on the notion of a hermeneutical-communitarian idea of the self – an idea which, for almost 300 years, had guided the idea of Afrikaners and their link with the idea of South Africa.

This powerful internal and external criticism, as well as more material influences such as sanctions, brought the NP – and the whole establishment of cultural, religious and civil organisations and institutions within its orbit – to the negotiating table in the early 1990s. The choice for Afrikaner elites in 1994, in strong alliance

---

[13] This, though, does not mean that the unitarian idea of South Africa overcomes the challenges of a plural society that in hindsight apartheid sought to address in such a misguided way. As Michael Sandel writes: 'intolerance flourishes most where forms of life are dislocated, roots unsettled, traditions undone. In our day, the totalitarian impulse has sprung less from the convictions of confidently situated selves than from the confusions of atomized, dislocated, frustrated selves, at sea in a world where common meanings have lost their force. As Hannah Arendt has written: "What makes mass society so difficult to bear is not the number of people involved, or at least not primarily, but the fact that the world between them has lost its power to gather them together, to relate and to separate them"' (1984): 7.

with the English speakers, was for negative freedom in the form of a rights-based and free market society: for the freedom and rights of the unencumbered individual protected within a liberal democratic constitution. Quite ironically, this was exactly the point at which another movement of collective positive freedom – that of African nationalism – came into state power.

A continuing tradition?

It is interesting that, despite the massive revolt of Afrikaner elites and a great deal of its upper middle class, the hermeneutical-communitarian idea of the self, so prominent in the past 300 years of Afrikaner history, has not come to an end. This tradition today survives both at political institutional level in the form of the Solidarity movement and in the work of a variety of public intellectuals. Solidarity is a remarkable trade union movement, led by Flip Buys, and it focuses predominantly on the economic and cultural position of Afrikaners as a minority group in South Africa. In many ways it embodies institutionally many elements of the older hermeneutical-encumbered position on the self as earlier explicated in the reconstruction of Afrikaner intellectual history. When it comes to the work of intellectuals, the following four figures can be considered: poet/thinker N.P. van Wyk Louw (1906–1970); political philosopher Johan Degenaar (born 1926); historian Hermann Giliomee (born 1938); and philosopher Danie Goosen (born 1953).

Louw is a complex poet and thinker – a *Dichter* in the German sense. In one of his best-known publications on liberal nationalism, *Liberale Nasionalisme*, which was written in 1958, he writes, 'No people should feel themselves on the fringes, far from the spontaneous-creative power of a centre outside themselves; every national culture is a self-centre; when it is derivative, it is only through its own choice and not because of the fate of its location or military weakness'

(1986: 413).[14] Although Louw refers to Afrikaners in nationalist terms, he claims that every people has a creative centre, but does not seek to interpret it in chauvinistic terms: he is interested in open dialogue or discussion – he called it *oop gesprek* – that is essential for any culture in and of itself, and in communication with other cultures. Eventually, he pleads for a kind of dialectical relation between individual (liberalism) and group (nationalism) – and introduces the concept of *liberale nasionalisme* (liberal nationalism), which operates in the same register as Sandel's notion of an encumbered self.

Johan Degenaar developed the concept of political pluralism from the 1970s following a lifelong interest in (and defence of) non-fundamentalist thinking and politics. Degenaar's early thinking was on liberalism and nationalism but, in the 1970s, it later expanded to include Marxism and black consciousness. Degenaar investigated the appropriateness of these ideas for South Africa, eventually settling on the idea of political pluralism, which he defended in various essays. Degenaar defines pluralism in a similar vein to Sandel, as a 'political philosophy that describes and prescribes value to the fact that man in society is *not* an isolated individual, but still acts in a plurality of groups. Groups here mean a great variety that come down to the following classes: peoples, cultural groups, communities, associations, organizations, institutes' (1980: 110).[15] It is plain that Degenaar does not see the idea of negative freedom – with its individualist rights-based ethic – as the only solution to South Africa's social challenges.

---

[14] My translation of: 'Geen volk hoef homself te voel as randgebied, as ver van die spontaan-skeppende krag van 'n sentrum buitekant homself nie; elke nasionale kultuur is self sentrum, wanneer hy derivatief is, is dit alleen deur sy eie keuse, nie deur die noodlot van sy ligging of weens militêre swakheid nie.'

[15] My translation of: 'Dit is 'n politieke filosofie waardeur (deskriptief) beskryf en (preskriptief) waarde geheg word aan die feit dat die mens in die samelewing nie as geïsoleerde individu nie, maar steeds binne 'n pluraliteit van groepe optree. Groeperinge dui op 'n groot gevarieerdheid en kan op die volgende klasse slaan: volke, kultuurgroepe, gemeenskappe, assosiasies, organisasies, institute.'

Hermann Giliomee makes a similar point in a recent interview.[16] After dealing with the question of minorities and majorities, he proceeds by problematising both liberalism and Marxism as ideological answers in a pluralist and divided society.[17] When it comes to liberals, Giliomee (2008: 536–537) thinks, first, that they 'have been very naïve in believing the ANC talk that it is a non-racial movement. I have always argued that it is a nationalist movement, using non-racialism only in winning and consolidating power'. Second, he thinks that liberals, just like Marxists, 'over-emphasise material interests' – whether this is based on the individual (as liberals think) or class (as Marxists think). Giliomee then turns to nationalists, and stresses that for them:

> *the struggle is about nationhood, about cultural identity and about relative group status. The programme of nationalists is to establish a viable community. It does not of course neglect economic concerns but the Afrikaner nationalists always tried to make certain that a certain class does not hijack the movement. Because liberals and Marxists put such emphasis on material interests they think that South African voters would shift from identity concerns to material concerns in choosing their party. They will wait for a long time.*

More recently, Danie Goosen has continued the work of Louw, Degenaar and Giliomee in his thinking about the position of Afrikaners as a minority group in a democratic South Africa. His major work on

---

[16] For his recent work on the last Afrikaner apartheid leaders, see Giliomee (2012).

[17] On the position of minorities and majorities in present-day South Africa, Giliomee says: 'The ANC does not subscribe to a pluralist conception of history or politics but to the Jacobin kind in which there is only room for an individual-based mass democracy, one where individuals are protected as long as they do not insist on minority protection, one where they constantly press English as language of instruction on Afrikaans schools and universities regardless of the damage it does ... It reminds one of the observation by Alexis de Tocqueville that minorities can only become part of the majority if they abandon the things that are really important to them and that create conflict between them and the majority' (2008): 540.

nihilism (2007) is an ambitious project to show how the concept of a hermeneutical-encumbered self has a long history reaching back to Aristotle and the Greeks.

In coming to a close, it must be restated that this presentation is *an* interpretation, not *the* interpretation, of Afrikaner intellectual history. Any suggestion to the contrary is mischief-making. True to Gadamer, no understanding is without prejudice and the challenge is to deal with our various prejudices. This conceded, this contribution has attempted to show how Afrikaners, in a variety of ways, have tried – and continue to try – to meet the central challenge of South African society, namely how to live with diversity. To do so has led to an intellectual tradition that is positioned between the two extremes that always tempt those who hold power in South Africa; that is, to overemphasise either difference or similarity. Notwithstanding the ultimate failure of Afrikaner state-nationalism, the question remains: What can South Africans learn from the far older tradition in Afrikaner intellectual history?

References

Anderson, B. (1983) *Imagined Communities: Reflections on the Origin and Spread of Nationalism*. London: Verso.

Aristotle (2009) *The Nicomachean Ethics*; translated by D. Ross and introduced by L. Brown. Oxford: OUP.

Berlin, I. (1984) 'Two concepts of liberty'. In Sandel, M. *Liberalism and its Critics*. Oxford: Blackwell.

Blumer, H. (1964) 'Race prejudice as a sense of group position'. In Musuoka, J. and Valien, P. (eds) *Race Relations: Problems and Theory*. Chapel Hill: University of North Carolina Press.

Coetzee, J.M. (1988) *White Writing: On the Culture of Letters in South Africa*. New Haven: Yale University Press.

D'Assonville, V.E. (1999) *S.J. du Toit van die Paarl (1847–1911)*. Weltevredenpark: Marnix.

Davenport, T.R.H. (1966) *The Afrikaner Bond*. Cape Town: Oxford.

_____. (1977) *South Africa: A Modern History*. Johannesburg: Macmillan.

De Klerk, W.A. (1976) *The Puritans in Africa: A Story of Afrikanerdom*. London: Pelican.

Degenaar, J.J. (1980) 'Staat en samelewing binne pluralistiese model'. In *Voortbestaan en Geregtigheid*. Cape Town: Tafelberg.

Diamond, J. (2005) *Collapse: How Societies Choose to Fail or to Succeed*. New York: Penguin.

Du Toit, A. and Giliomee, H. (1983) *Afrikaner Political Thought: Analysis and Documents: Volume I: 1780–1850*. Cape Town: David Phillip.

Duvenage, P. (2013) 'Praktiese wysheid (fronesis) in 'n verdeelde samelewing'. *Litnet Akademies* 10(2): 577–601.

Gadamer, H.G. (1960) *Wahrheit und Methode*. Tübingen: Mohr Siebeck.

_____. (2004) *Truth and Method*; translated by J. Weinsheimer and D.G. Marshall. London: Continuum, 2nd ed.

Giliomee, H. (1975) 'Die ontwikkeling van selfkonsepsies by die Afrikaner'. In Van der Merwe, H.W. (ed.). *Identiteit en Verandering: Sewe Opstelle oor die Afrikaner Vandag*. Cape Town: Tafelberg.

_____. (2004) *Die Afrikaners: 'N Biografie*. Cape Town: Tafelberg (published in English as *The Afrikaners: Biography of a People*, 2003).

_____. (2008) '"An historian of Afrikaner origin, but not an Afrikaner historian": Hermann Giliomee at 70: interview with Heribert Adam'. *South African Historical Journal* 60(4): 535–561.

_____. (2012) *The Last Afrikaner Leaders: A Supreme Test of Power*. Cape Town: NB Publishers.

Goosen, D. (2007) *Nihilisme*. Johannesburg: Praag Uitgewers.

Holiday, A. (1993) 'Conversations in a colony: natural language and primitive interchange'. *Pretexts* 4(2): 3–19.

Honneth, A. (1995) *The Struggle for Recognition: The Moral Grammar of Social Conflicts*. Cambridge: Polity Press.

Kestell, J.D. (1911) *Het Leven van Professor N.J. Hofmeyr*. Cape Town: HAUM.

Louw, N.P.v.W. (1986) 'Liberale nasionalisme'. In *Versamelde Prosa I*. Cape Town: Tafelberg.

Mentzel, O.F. (1919) *Life at the Cape in the Mid-Eighteenth Century*. Cape Town: Van Riebeeck Society.

Moodie, D. (1975) *The Rise of Afrikanerdom: Power, Apartheid, and the Afrikaner Civil Religion*. Berkeley: University of California Press.

Murray, A.H. (1947) 'Die Afrikaner se wysgerige denke'. In Van den Heever, C.M. and Pienaar, P.deV. *Kultuurgeskiedenis van die Afrikaner: Deel II*. Cape Town: Nasionale Boekhandel.

Nash, A. (2009) *The Dialectical Tradition in South Africa*. New York: Routledge.

Norval, A. (1996) *Deconstructing Apartheid Discourse*. London: Verso.

O'Meara, D. (1983) *Volkskapitalisme: Class, Capital, and Ideology in the

Development of Afrikaner Nationalism 1934–1948. Johannesburg: Ravan Press.

_____ (1996) *Forty Lost Years: The Apartheid State and the Politics of the National Party, 1948–1994*. Johannesburg: Ravan Press.

Sandel, M. (1982) *Liberalism and the Limits of Justice*. Cambridge: Cambridge University Press.

_____ (2009) *Justice: What is the Right Thing to Do?* New York: Farrar, Straus and Giroux.

Sandel, M. (ed.) (1984) *Liberalism and Its Critics*. Oxford: Blackwell.

Schoeman, K. (1997) *Dogter van Sion: Machteld Smit en die Agtiende-Eeuse Samelewing aan die Kaap, 1749–1799*. Cape Town: Human and Rousseau.

_____. (2013) *Portrait of a Slave Society: The Cape of Good Hope 1717–1795*. Pretoria: Protea Publishers.

Schoeman, M.J. (1983) 'Hermeneutiek en die geesteswetenskappe'. In Dreyer, P.S. (ed.) *Objek en Metode in die Geesteswetenskappe*. Pretoria: University of Pretoria Press.

Scholtz, G.D. (1967–1979) *Die Ontwikkeling van die Politieke Denke van die Afrikaner: Volumes I–V*. Johannesburg: Voortrekkerpers and Perskor.

Van Jaarsveld, F.A. (1981) *Wie en Wat is die Afrikaner?* Cape Town: Tafelberg.

Warnke, G. (1987) *Gadamer, Hermeneutics, Tradition and Reason*. Cambridge: Polity Press.

Wessels, J. (2010) 'ANC, onthou om te onthou'. *Beeld* 9 April.

Wright, G. (1998) 'Gadamer'. In Craig, C. (ed.). *Routledge Encyclopaedia of Philosophy*. London: Routledge.

The hidden histories of Afrikaans

HEIN WILLEMSE

For Tienie du Plessis (1949–2015)

1.

Afrikaans is an African language, with its primary speech community concentrated on the African continent. Afrikaans is a southern African language. Today, six in ten of the almost seven million Afrikaans speakers in South Africa are estimated to be black (in the generic sense of the word), a figure that will by all indications increase significantly in the next decade. Like several other South African languages, Afrikaans is a cross-border language spanning sizable communities of speakers in Namibia, Botswana and Zimbabwe. In South Africa and Namibia Afrikaans is spoken across all social indices, by the poor and the rich, by rural and urban people, by the undereducated and the educated. Afrikaans is a creole language. It shares traits common to creolised languages in the Caribbean, the Malayan Peninsula, Indonesia, the northern parts of South America, and an East African Niger-Congo (or Bantu) creole like KiSwahili.

In this contribution to the MISTRA round-table discussion, I have chosen to concentrate on reminding us of the varied history of the Afrikaans language. I focus mostly on the black history of

Afrikaans rather than the known hegemonic history inculcated by Afrikaner nationalist education, propaganda and the media. In the debate on language and culture we often hear only the Afrikaner Christian National version of the story of Afrikaans, but its history is a multi-faceted one to which many South Africans of every hue have contributed. While our recent socio-political history often casts Afrikaans as the language of racists, oppressors and unreconstructed nationalists, the language also bears the imprint of a fierce tradition of anti-imperialism, anti-colonialism, of an all-embracing humanism and anti-apartheid activism.

2.
In 1860, one of the students in a Cape Town madrasah, a descendant of slaves, copied a prayer into his exercise book. Today the surviving fragments of that book reveal a history that somehow remains hidden from the vast majority of South Africans. The exercises in that book, also called a *koplesboek*,[1] are written in Cape Malay dialect, the colloquial language of the time:[2] 'waarliek ouai ies ghapierais ien ies ghoeroet ... Ja Allah viermeerdie ouai bramataghait ... op Moegammad ien op sain faamielghie ... niet soewals ouai ghiedaan hiet op Nabee Iebraheem'. In English translation this passage reads: 'truly Thou art praised and elevated ... O God increase Thy blessings ... on Muhammed and on his family ... just as Thou had done for Prophet Abraham' (Davids, 2011: 114). Apart from the pseudo-phonetic spelling, any contemporary Afrikaans speaker would recognise this as near-modern Afrikaans, in this case written in Arabic script.

---

[1] The *koplesboek* refers to the notebook in which students committed their exercises to writing and from which they memorised their school work – see Davids (2011): 67.

[2] For the concept Cape Malay dialect see Rochlin in Davids (2011): 89.

The hidden histories of Afrikaans

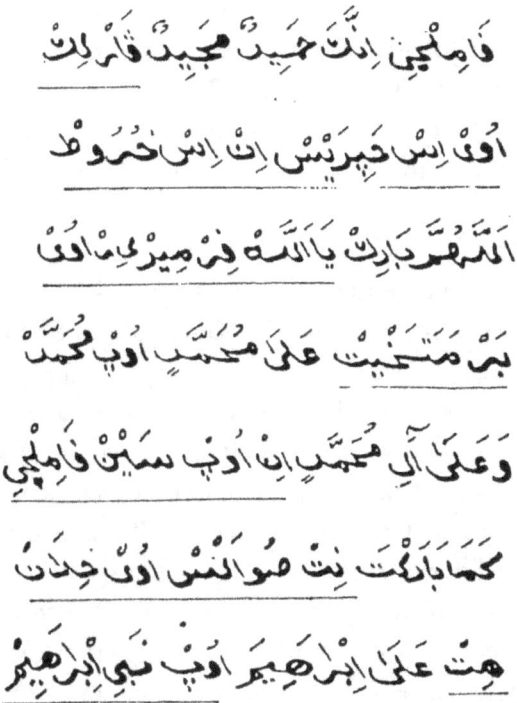

This is but one example of a well-known tradition of *a'jami* scripts produced in the Cape Muslim community in the latter half of the nineteenth century and well into the 1950s. In fact, the exercise book that I have cited is not the oldest known copy of a *koplesboek*. Achmat Davids found a similar *koplesboek* dating back to 1806 (Davids, 2011: 70). To give some historical perspective: this was as early as the time of the second British occupation of the Cape Colony, or when Shaka was a young man of 19 on the verge of his evolution into a notable military leader. The best-known of these Arabic-Afrikaans texts is Abubaker Effendi's *Bay n al-Din*, a guidebook to Islam, among the oldest books in Afrikaans, completed in 1867 and printed ten years later in Constantinople, Turkey.[3] Arabic-Afrikaans was used not only in religious texts but also in daily communication,

---

[3] The unavailability of an appropriate printing press that could handle publications in Arabic script clearly influenced Effendi's decision to have the book published in Constantinople (Davids, 2011: 89, 115ff).

the making of shopping lists, political pamphlets, or, in the case of the politician Achmat Effendi, in a letter to a friend following his defeat in an election for a seat in the Cape Parliament in 1894 (Davids, 2011: 19, 93–97). For the Cape Muslims, a literate community, this language was the bearer of their most intimate thoughts and their religion.

Visitors and immigrants to the Cape, such as Arnoldus Pannevis, M.D. Teenstra and Hubertus Elffers, on their arrival quickly realised that 'the best representatives of Cape Dutch are to be found among the Malay population of the Cape Peninsula ... and the Bastards born and bred at German mission stations where Cape Dutch forms the only medium of expression' (Elffers quoted in Davids, 2011: 86–87).[4] Off-shoots of the latter community of speakers were those who self-identified as Oorlams, Griquas or Bastaards. Cape Dutch was disseminated during the late 1780s and early 1800s to the north-western Cape Colony, today's west coast of the Northern Cape and southern Namibia. It is commonly accepted that the Oorlams, i.e. the descendants of Cape Khoekhoen groups, migrated to these parts, spreading their mother tongue, Cape Dutch, to the arid regions on both sides of the Gariep (Orange) River. Along with early trekboere and the Rehobothers, i.e. descendants of Khoekhoen and European liaisons, who generally self-identify as Bastaards or Basters, the Oorlams (with leaders such as Jonker Afrikaner, David Christiaan and Moses Witbooi) played a major role in the establishment of Cape Dutch as the language of trade, culture and education during the late-1800s and early twentieth century (see Groenewald, 2010; Stals and Ponelis, 2011: 71; Stell, 2009: 86).

However, not everyone thought that the simplified, creolised speech, with its roots mainly in Dutch, the seafarer variants of Malay, Portuguese, Indonesian and the indigenous Khoekhoen and San languages, could express learning, writing or upper middle class culture. Whether known as Cape Dutch, Cape Malay, Hotnotstaal,

---

[4] For an example of the Cape Dutch on the Moravian mission stations, see Jerzy Koch (2015): 241–271.

Hottentots-Hollands, Kitchen-Dutch, mongrel Dutch or Afrikaa,[5] this creole language, spoken by the peasants, the urban proletariat, whatever their ethnic background, and even the middle class of civil servants, traders and teachers, was derided by the upper classes of the Cape Colony, be they Dutch- or English-speaking, in the nineteenth century. The opinion of Chief Justice Lord J.H. de Villiers (quoted in Giliomee, 2003: 216) was that this language was 'poor in the number of its words, weak in its inflections, wanting in accuracy of meaning'. Such opinions were representative of views that speech and intelligence were somehow connected, and that Cape Dutch was thought to be 'incapable of expressing ideas connected with the higher spheres of thought'. From the Cape Dutch-speaking (white) middle class came the pushback that sought to disprove and counter such elite perceptions.

Around 1870, the first steps towards the battle between various views on the nature of Cape Dutch, or what would become known as Afrikaans, were taken. Some of the leading figures of what would become known as the 'first language movement' (1874–1890) strenuously denied the creole nature of the language. For them Afrikaans was 'a pure Germanic language', a *landstaal* (national language), and a language of 'purity, simplicity, brevity and vigor' (quoted in Giliomee, 2003: 217). The Genootskap van Regte Afrikaanders (GRA, the Society of True Afrikaners), established in 1875 at Paarl, actively sought to foster a nationalism among white Cape Dutch-speakers: Afrikaans became their linguistic vehicle and 'Afrikaners' their label. They (and their eventual successors) sought to write a nationalist history of oppressors and victims, establishing the beginnings of a print nationalism with their booklets of children's tales, nationalist poetry and publications (Giliomee, 2003: 217–220).

The three instances cited above – the commitment of Cape Dutch

---

[5] Abdurahim Muhammed al Iraki compiled his extraordinary glossary *'n Vaiftalige Woordelais en Kort Sinnetjies in Arab, Farsi, Hinistani, Afrikaa en Engels* (Bombay: Kalzar Husna, 1905), in which the name 'Afrikaa' referred to the language Afrikaans (Davids, 2011: 139). Davids observes that Cape Muslims at the time 'regarded themselves as "Afferkaners"' and their language as 'Afrikaa' (ibid.).

to Arabic script, the migration of the language into the north-western Cape Colony and the establishment of the GRA – are illustrative of processes of organic language expansion. These three communities of Cape Dutch-speakers reacted very differently to the expansion of their common tongue. The imams of the Cape formulated among themselves appropriate ways of writing the language and making it accessible to the faithful, at one point even changing to Roman script to accommodate new adherents – mostly young white women – to the faith (Davids, 2011: 209ff). The Oorlams were outward-looking and regarded Cape Dutch as a bridge between communities rather than their exclusive domain and used it without any obvious political intent. The first two groupings did not seek to mould a language, common to the Cape's lower and middle classes, into a possession but used it as a resource of communication and outreach. None of them, except the ethnic entrepreneurs, the nationalists of the GRA, sought to actively demarcate their language to the point of diminishing and stigmatising other speakers' claim to it, declaring their own version of Cape Dutch as prestige Burger Afrikaans, the distinct 'white man's language'.

The imams of the Cape actively modified and standardised the writing of Afrikaans in Arabic script. Achmat Davids' major contribution to Afrikaans language studies is indeed his elaboration of the orthographic innovation these men brought about in their representation of spoken Afrikaans in the last quarter of the nineteenth century. Looking back at Afrikaans historically, there is much to be said for the dogged manner in which the early Afrikaner language nationalists and their successors modified a spoken language. Like the imams, they took an unscripted argot and forged it into a written script. The early nationalists standardised a creole even if denied, and through their activism forged it into a modern (Romanised) written language. They used a common patois, and in the face of prejudice chose to ennoble it, using written Dutch as the basis for its codification. Yet the racial prejudice and middle-class bias underlying many of their choices had far-reaching implications. In denying the commonality of their fellow Afrikaans speakers who were descendants of slaves, indigenous people or simply poor, they were elevating the language to a narrow ethnic nationalist cause. Through a web of actions and policies that influenced education, cultural and economic policies well into the twentieth century, Afrikaans was constructed as a white language, with a white history and white faces.

From early on, the divide between linguists who advanced views that suggested that Afrikaans was a creole and those denying this assumption, became fiercely contested. D.C. Hesseling argued in his pioneering study *Het Afrikaansch* (1899) that the language was indeed 'mixed', while D.B. Bosman in *Oor die ontstaan van Afrikaans* (1916) argued equally strongly that Afrikaans is 'no mixed language, certainly not a mixed language that originated with Dutch speaking the Malay-Portuguese of the slaves'; and that its structure and vocabulary were due to 'spontaneous evolution' (quoted in Willemse, 2012: 69). Hesseling's theory of Afrikaans as a creole language fell into disrepute, its advocates were ridiculed and for much of the twentieth century learners and students were dissuaded from supporting such views. I and other researchers have pointed out that Afrikaans-language textbooks after 1948 promoted Afrikaans development as a myth and actively co-created an Afrikaner nationalist paradigm (Esterhuyse, 1986; Willemse, 1992c; Willemse, 2012).

Notwithstanding their fancy theories and their wide acceptance within university, college and school curricula, Bosman and his followers could not deny the language's creolity. For example, Neville Alexander tells an interesting, illustrative anecdote in an interview that surprisingly sheds light on the language and its creole history. As a student in Germany during the 1950s, Alexander and his international friends often sang folk songs together, and he continues:

> One day they asked me to sing something from Cape Town and I sang 'Suikerbossie', 'Sugarbush', a very simple little song. When I was sort of getting into it, the Indonesian said, 'Stop, but that's not a Cape Town song, that's our song.' I said, 'What do you mean, it's your song? No, I'm singing in Afrikaans.' And he said, 'No, that's an Indonesian song.' So I thought well, there must be an explanation, and the only explanation I can think of is that it came with the slaves. It was funny because he

was outraged – *'How can you claim the song for yourself, it's our song'*; and I said, *'As far as I know it is our song'* (Alexander in Busch et al, 2014: 66).

This is not the forum in which to discuss the intricacies of the various theories save to state that by the late-1980s the spontaneous evolution theory was largely on the retreat. Today, the creole language theory is in the ascendancy. The leading linguists in this respect are mostly non-South Africans, among them the Dutch author, the late Hans den Besten (2012). He convincingly proved that Portuguese Creole, Malay varieties, and most significantly, Khoekhoen, played a significant role in the formation of the language. He even argued that were it not for the agency of the 'indigenous Khoekhoen and imported African and Asian slave labor … there would be no Afrikaans' (quoted in Van Rensburg, 2012). Considering the dominance for much of the twentieth century of the spontaneous evolution theory, this point of view is as close to heresy as it gets.

3.

The construction of language as 'an international language', or 'a tribal language', or 'a language of love', or 'a language of the oppressor', has little to do with the language itself. It says more about the social environment where language serves as a metaphor for a variety of ideas, images, aspirations, emotions, orientations, and, most crucially, economic, political and social power. One of the major ways in which colonialism affected the subjugated is the denial of their being, their psyche: often the subjugated see themselves as becoming fully human only when they act or behave like the colonialists, i.e. to imitate their speech, their institutions and their behaviour. Often people formulate an anti-colonialist stance countering such colonial institutions. In the past century, the development of language policy and institutions often reflected such perspectives.

When the Afrikaner nationalists came to power in 1948, they brought with them a set of ideas about society, social organisation, the economy, culture and language that had developed over the preceding century, under the direction of successive waves of nationalist thought.

Among these decisions was the introduction of mother-tongue education, which in progressive societies would have been a signal of independence, the empowerment of vast numbers of indigenous speakers; and a certain sign of postcolonial achievement. However, under apartheid rule language was deployed as a tool of tribalism, in the service of the divide-and-rule policy, and, instead of a sign of empowerment, it became a marker of under- and mis-education. One of the unintended consequences of the apartheid policy and Bantu Education was the level of self-loathing that speakers developed around indigenous languages, which they perceived as having little or no value in a contemporary business or educational environment.

Contrast, in this regard, the situation of Afrikaans. In the first half of the twentieth century the language had developed into an impressive anti-imperial achievement in terms of its codification; the development of its literature; the modernisation of wide-ranging language resources, from subject and general dictionaries to increasing numbers of language educators; the establishment of cultural and language institutes; and the development of printing and media industries. By the time the nationalists came to political power in 1948, the position of Afrikaans was further bolstered and it gained a foothold in all sectors of society, including the civil service and the economy. In a disastrous policy decision, the Department of Bantu Education enforced its 50–50 (50 per cent Afrikaans–50 per cent English) language policy, thereby imposing Afrikaans as a language of instruction on non-Afrikaans speakers. The impact of such coercive power on Afrikaans was the point of ignition for the uprising of 1976, and along with it suspicion of its speakers.

The advancement of Afrikaans in the twentieth century, mostly under the aegis of Afrikaner nationalism, meant that the other constituent histories and stories of the language and its speakers were either neglected or suppressed. Rather than viewing Afrikaans through a single lens, it is today acknowledged as an amalgam consisting of a variety of expressions, speakers and histories. For example, historical linguists often base their research on the meticulous exploration of texts and corpora, which prejudices the illiterate and those who do not produce or retain written traces of their lives in language. Quite often, those people on the margins only find their way into history through the gateways of state institutions, be it the courts, prisons or the passages of a health system. Increasingly, black speakers are demanding the re-standardisation of their language, the recognition of regional varieties and the collection and acknowledgement of their linguistic and cultural expressions, taking into account alternative ways of gathering information and the acknowledgement of alternative histories (Van den Heever, 1988; Hendricks, 2012; Willemse, 2012). One such history is the history of resistance.[6]

Permit me some self-indulgence to illustrate my point. I took the decision to study the Afrikaans language, literature and culture in its fullness in the wake of the tragic events of the second half of 1976. It was a decision rooted in the uprisings in which Afrikaans was labelled 'the language of the oppressor'. The slogan was rightly an emotive, visceral response to Afrikaner ethnic, nationalist hegemony and its concomitant coercive state power, but it also obscured the experiences, lives and histories of black and non-nationalist Afrikaans speakers. To my mind, we needed to understand language (in this instance Afrikaans) not only as a matter of racial and tribal construction but also, at base, as a matter of social class.

Up to that time in my life I had lived in small towns in the southern and western regions of the then Cape Province, in the southern Cape, the Boland, the Little Karoo. By the time I was eighteen, I was fortunate to have travelled north to the Northern Cape, to the Free State, Natal and Transvaal, and even further to Botswana, Mozambique and Rhodesia. On those travels I had witnessed deep poverty in isolated rural homesteads. The people that I met in the far-flung villages of today's southern Namibia and Northern Cape were as desperately poor as I had seen elsewhere, and they were mostly Afrikaans-speaking. How could they, these people – the poorest of the poor – be 'the oppressor'? Why were their stories not told? How could those people struggling in the townships of the towns that I've lived in, or the people in Cape Town's townships where I helped out

---

[6] See my articles in *Mayibuye*, where these matters have been discussed for a popular readership.

as a para-legal in the University of the Western Cape's (UWC) student law society, be 'the oppressor'? Why were their stories not told?

In 1976, UWC became the hub of the student uprising in the Western Cape and we as students sang revolutionary songs in *isiXhosa*, English and Afrikaans (Thomas, 1997). We performed plays and poetry in Afrikaans; and a young, eloquent firebrand named Allan Boesak whipped us all into rousing black consciousness fervour – in Afrikaans.[7] This is an example of Afrikaans in resistance; it is also an example of a counter-narrative unknown to those outside the sphere of Afrikaans speakers. There are many such tales in the distant past – and even closer to our time.

One of the undoubted successes of Afrikaner nationalist hegemony was the creation of the myth that the nationalists, and only they, spoke for those identified as Afrikaners, and that their world view was the only significant expression of being Afrikaans-speaking. Not only did nationalist functionaries and culture brokers suppress opposition and alternative thought within the Afrikaner community, they also minimised the role and place of black Afrikaans speakers in the broader speech community. In all of this, language historians, nationalist politicians, the media and school curricula have chosen to tell one story, and it was this story that non-Afrikaans speakers – individuals, communities and institutions outside the Afrikaans speech community – have accepted as the only story. Afrikaans became indelibly identified with Afrikaner nationalism – with the oppressor.

In the process, the place and relevance of black Afrikaans speakers have been denied. The constituent sides of the broader Afrikaans-speaking community, of black Afrikaans-speaking people in particular, today's numerical majority, have been silenced effectively. As young, black-consciousness-inspired academics, we understood that a different story needed to be told – at the very least one that tells of a more encompassing history, a history that explored the life and culture of those marginalised, i.e. the neglected histories, language,

---

[7] Jonathan Jansen (2007) said of that experience: 'I was never so entranced in my life as when Allan Boesak, mainly in Afrikaans, spoke to the growing anger and resentment that I felt as a black person' (128).

literature and culture of black Afrikaans speakers.

At UWC, where I was appointed in 1979, we increasingly came to understand our historical duty to write up the silent and silenced histories of Afrikaans. Our curriculum in Afrikaans studies at UWC, like elsewhere, initially reflected very little of any significance of the history of black Afrikaans speakers, their culture or their literature. By 1987 we had gradually reshaped the UWC curriculum to include black authors and introduced language dialect studies, which included the study of black Afrikaans speech. That department, at one point the largest department of Afrikaans, contributed to reshaping academic thinking around Afrikaans literature and language, and, along with a younger generation of linguists elsewhere, increasingly explored the language's diverse and vibrant history (De Jong, 1989; Hendricks, 1978; Links, 1989; Van de Rheede, 1983; Smith et al., 1986; Willemse, 1999; Willemse et al., 1997; Willemse and Van Wyk, 2015).

Throughout the apartheid era and the dominance of what André Brink once called 'Apartaans', the other (non-Afrikaner nationalist Afrikaans) stories have continued to exist (Brink in Van den Heever, 1988). Here, I have elected to focus on the lesser-known side of language and literature studies, but there continue to exist hidden histories of Afrikaans-speaking people in many other spheres of South African life, be it as cultural expression, in the worker movement, in the media or, perhaps more spectacularly, in reformed theology, where the very ethos of anti-apartheid and liberation theology was shaped by black Afrikaans-speaking theologians.

4.

Today Afrikaner nationalism has been severely diminished and, along with it, the standing of Afrikaans in the public sector. Nonetheless, in the private spheres of culture, private education, the media and subscription television, Afrikaans has seen an exponential growth. As suggested earlier, the very nature of contemporary Afrikaans, the white-speaker bias of its media products and dominant institutions, remain under constant discussion, and we still have to recognise the multi-faceted nature of the Afrikaans-speaking community, the numerical dominance of its black speakers, and the need to advance Afrikaans in a multilingual, all-inclusive, antiracist environment, as an example and as part of the development and intellectualisation of African languages. We also have to recognise that Afrikaans is at the core of many fellow South Africans' sense of identity, and that they are not necessarily white. It is in this spirit that the debate on the medium of instruction at universities such as Stellenbosch has to be conducted. It is obvious that the administrators and the constituent bodies at that institution have to find ways to continue to advance Afrikaans without the perceptions and experiences of racist behaviour associated with early and ruling Afrikaner nationalist practices. Our sense of diversity in our nationhood will have to be forged, so that all South Africans will see themselves reflected in our public sphere.

References

Busch, B., Busch, L. and Press, K. (eds) (2014) *Interviews with Neville Alexander: The Power of Languages Against the Language of Power*. Pietermaritzburg: University of KwaZulu-Natal Press.

Davids, A. (2012) In *The Afrikaans of the Cape Muslims* edited by Willemse, H. and Dangor, S. E. Pretoria: Protea Boekhuis.

De Jong, M. (1989) *'N Ander Afrikaanse Letterkunde: Marxistiese en Sosiaalgerigte Teksopvattings in Afrikaans*. Pretoria: Human Sciences Research Council.

Esterhuyse, J. (1986) *Taalapartheid en Skoolafrikaans*. Emmarentia: Taurus.

Giliomee, H. (2003) *The Afrikaner: Biography of a People*. Cape Town: Tafelberg.

Groenewald, G. (2010) 'Afrikaans as lingua franca in Namibië, ca. 1800–1920'. *LitNet Akademies* 7(3), available at http://www.litnet.co.za/afrikaans-as-lingua-franca-in-namibie/.

Hendricks, F.S. (1978) 'Sinchronies-diachroniese studie van die taalgebruik in die drama Kanna hy kô hystoe van Adam Small'. MA thesis, University of the Western Cape.

Hendricks, F. (2012) 'The potential advantage of an egalitarian view of the varieties of Afrikaans'. In Prah, Kwesi Kwaa (ed.). *Mainstreaming Afrikaans Regional Varieties*. Rondebosch: Centre for Advanced Studies of African Society: 43–62.

Jansen, J. (2007) 'King James, Princess Alice and the ironed hair: a tribute to Stephen Bantu Biko'. In Van Wyk, C. (ed.). *We Write What We Like: Celebrating Steve Biko*. Johannesburg: Wits University Press.

Koch, J. (2015) *A History of South African Literature: Afrikaans Literature 17th–19th Centuries*. Pretoria: Van Schaik.

Links, T. (1989) *So Praat ons Namakwalanders*. Cape Town: Tafelberg.

Smith, J. F., Van Gensen, A. and Willemse, H. (eds) (1986) *Swart Afrikaanse Skrywers: Verslag van 'n Simposium Gehou by die Universiteit van Wes-Kaapland, Bellville, op 26–27 April 1985*. Bellville: University of Western Cape.

Stals, E.L.P. and Ponelis, F. (2001) *Só het Afrikaans na Namibië Gekom*. Windhoek: Gamsberg Macmillan.

Stell, G. (2009) 'Is there a Namibian Afrikaans? Recent trends in grammatical variation in Afrikaans varieties within and across Namibia's borders'. *Stellenbosch Papers in Linguistics PLUS* 39: 85–105.

Thomas, C. C. (1997) *Wakker Wakker en aan die Brand*. Bellville: Mayibuye Books.

Van de Rheede, I. (1983) ''N Sosiolinguistiese ondersoek na taalgebruik in Bellville-Suid'. MA thesis, University of the Western Cape.

Van den Heever, R. (1988) *Afrikaans en Bevryding. Alternatiewe Afrikaans*. Kasselsvlei: Cape Professional Teachers' Union.

Van der Wouden, T. (2012) *Roots of Afrikaans: Selected Writings of Hans den Besten*. Amsterdam: John Benjamins.

Van Rensburg, C. (2012) 'Afrikaans lekker ná skep uit baie tale'. *Beeld* 4 September available at www.beeld.com/MyBeeld/Briewe/Afrikaans-lekker-na-skep-uit-baie-tale-20120904.

Willemse, H. (1992a) 'Afrikaans: a white man's language?' *Mayibuye* 3(8): 29–32.

_____. (1992b) 'Afrikaans writers: the anti-apartheid tradition'. *Mayibuye* 3(9): 29–32.

_____. (1992c) 'Securing the myth: the representation of the origins of Afrikaans in school language textbooks'. In Jansen, J. (ed.) *Knowledge and Power in South Africa: Critical Perspectives Across the Disciplines*. Johannesburg: Skotaville: 249–263.

_____. (1999) ''N inleiding tot buitekanonieke Afrikaanse kulturele praktyke'. In Van Coller, H.P. (ed.). *Perspektief en Profiel: 'N Afrikaanse Literatuurgeskiedenis*. Pretoria: Van Schaik, 2nd ed: 73–91.

_____. (2012) 'Considering a more multi-faceted Afrikaans'. In Prah, Kwesi Kwaa (ed.) *Mainstreaming Afrikaans Regional Varieties*. Rondebosch: Centre for Advanced Studies of African Society: 63–88.

Willemse, H. et al. (eds) (1997) *Die Reis na Paternoster*. Bellville: University of the Western Cape.

Willemse, H. and Van Wyk, S. (eds) (2015) *'N Vlag aan die Tong: Wilderness: Abrile Doman*. Pretoria: Hond.

A South African ('n Suid-Afrikaner) university
Is it possible?

NICO KOOPMAN

1.

South Africans are experts in diverse and apart, but a generation after the dawn of democracy we still have so much to learn about diverse and together.

2.

In South Africa and elsewhere we did not deal well with the gift of diversity. Of diversity we have made division, discrimination and dehumanisation. Ethnic diversity became racism; socio-economic diversity – classism; gender diversity – sexism; diversity with regard to sexual orientation – homophobia; with regard to age – ageism; with regard to different levels of ability – handicappism/able-ism; with regard to our relationship with the natural environment – ecocide; with regard to various church denominations – ecclesial isolation and anti-ecumenism; with regard to the relationship with other religions – religious alienation.

3.

These forms of discrimination have three dimensions. Let us take racism as an example.

First, subtle and even subconscious pictures/ideas/views of the other ethnic group that suggest the other is inferior or superior with regard to features like skin colour, hair texture, face shape, nose form, intellect, morality and the ability to enter into a relationship with God.

Second, social structures were erected that reflect these pictures and prejudices. South Africa did not invent racism, but we perfected it. The structures of macro- and micro-apartheid were perfect embodiments of the hierarchical, discriminative, dehumanising pictures and prejudices of racism.

Third, we developed sophisticated theological rationales for these pictures and their accompanying structures. The pseudo-gospel was proclaimed that apartheid was God's good news for South Africa. Apartheid was proclaimed as God's solution to South Africa's crisis of diversity. These pictures were God's pictures, and these structures, God's structures.

This threefold description of racism applies to all other forms of discrimination and dehumanisation.

4.

As South Africans we are working hard, by far not hard enough, to journey away from this painful reality of diverse and apart to a new reality of diverse and together, where we are freed from division, discrimination and dehumanisation.

5.

South African universities can strive to offer – through our research and innovation, teaching and learning, social impact and transformation, and through our co-curricular activities and professional support services – a threefold response to the threefold dimension of evils like racism.

Our journey from diverse and apart is a journey of conscientisation about the subtle pictures and prejudices with which we live. Therefore, ongoing prophetic and priestly exposures of the subtle forms of discrimination are crucial. This leads to an institutional culture, a collective personality and a communal character that bids farewell to division, discrimination and dehumanisation.

It is a journey of organising new structures that reflect dignity, cohesion and togetherness. Therefore, the creation of liberating decision-making structures and the transformation of our semiotics are crucial.

It is a journey of mobilising our spiritual and other resources to make racism and other evils history, and to go beyond them.

6.

On this journey away from racism towards reconciliation and justice we are challenged to deal with complexity with its various features, i.e. with plurality and ambiguity, with ambivalence and paradoxality, with duality and nuanced perspectives, and with absurdity.

A plurality of voices, opinions and perspectives on challenges like reconciliation and justice should be welcomed. These voices are manifold and more often than not contradictory. We need to accept this plurality and deal constructively with it through exposure of views to each other, through dialogue and the search for consensus, or even peaceful co-existence and continuous deliberations in the case of incommensurable and irreconcilable positions.

Ambiguity refers to the fact that the same phenomenon or reality can be described in different and even contradictory ways by different people and in different contexts. Ambiguity also refers to the shifting meanings of words, sentences and concepts. We more than often want to avoid ambiguity. People who cannot live with ambiguity choose either absolutism or relativism. Absolutism implies that only my interpretation, description and solution are right. Absolutism paves the way for judgementalism, fundamentalism, even some form of anti-intellectualism or irrationality, and also the stereotyping, stigmatisation, demonisation and annihilation of the other. Relativism, on the other hand, feeds an attitude of passivity, *acedia*, melancholy, pessimism, internal emigration and nihilism.

In our reconciliation and justice discourses we witness how either one of these two, absolutism or relativism, are the more popular options. To travel on the road of ambiguity asks for wisdom, courage and patience. It also asks for the ability to communicate very sophisticated positions in clear and intellectually accessible ways. Ambiguity should not be confused with lack of clarity and vagueness.

Reconciliation and justice quests also ask that we deal constructively with ambivalence. Ambivalence entails that we sometimes and in some senses make progress, and we sometimes and in some senses experience setbacks as well. We have beautiful stories to tell about our liberation from racism and of our victory over racism. We, however, also have stories to deal with about how we still experience mostly covert, but also overt, forms of racism. The same applies to other evils like classism, sexism, homophobia, able-ism, xenophobia and ecocide. To seek reconciliation and justice faithfully and responsibly, we need to acknowledge and live with this ambivalence. To serve reconciliation and justice, we need to hold on to both. We cannot absolutise one of the two only. We need to say, yes, there are good things happening in South Africa – otherwise we will become discouraged, melancholic, apathetic and *acedic*, and unfaithful to our God-given calling. And we need to say, yes, there are still bad things happening in South Africa – otherwise we will become unrealistic and naive, and we will be insensitive to the pain and anger in our society. With this ambivalence we need to live.

To address the challenging questions regarding reconciliation and justice we also need to live with paradoxality, i.e. with apparent but not real contradictions. Take the question of whether we should talk about the past as an example. Should we still continue to talk about the past? Yes, because if we do not talk about the past the unaddressed anger and pain, shame and guilt, will keep on haunting us. No, because if we do not stop talking about the past we might keep each other trapped in the past and foreclose the wonderful prospect of journeying together and energetically into the future. Or take another question: Do we need to refer to each other in colour categories? Yes, we need to do this for the sake of trying to make some reparation for wrongs that were done along colour lines for centuries, on condition that this is a fairly applied and interim arrangement, and as long as we also address other categories of injustice like those pertaining to gender, class, disability, age and the environment. No, because we need to avoid racial categorisation for the sake of working together to actualise the vision of a non-racial South Africa! Apparent contradictory responses to the same questions are the paradoxality that we need to live with, and with which universities should equip their graduates.

Duality is another feature of the complexity we need to live with in our journey towards reconciliation and justice. Thereby I mean the capacity to live with the notion of both, and not only with the more famous either/or. Some people, for instance, still think it is not possible to grow in excellence and diversity simultaneously. They reckon that to say yes to diversity implies that you say no to excellence. We need to arrive at the point where we recognise that it is not possible to claim excellence in a diversified society if you do not show hospitality to a diversity of persons, contexts, perspectives and ideas. No excellence without diversity is not an empty slogan.

We should also develop nuanced perspectives. In our own journey towards justice and reconciliation we should investigate the lessons that South Africans can learn from the quests for reconciliation, justice and transformation in other post-liberation struggle contexts like, among others, the post-South African War period, the post-World War II period in Germany, the post-civil rights struggle context in the United States, the post-liberation struggle context in Brazil, etc. This broader focus will shed more light on our own struggle. Thorough historical analyses and cross-national analyses of our own and other quests for reconciliation and justice will help us describe our own challenges in a more nuanced way. It will also help us find strength and hope from others who also struggle hard to actualise a good society of unity and reconciliation, justice and peace. Moreover, it helps to develop the right emotional orientation and sensitivity for our local challenges. It might free us from both the over-sensitivity and the un-sensitivity that form stumbling blocks on the road to peace.

The last feature of complexity has to do with a logic that seems to be absurd, ridiculous and foolish. For reconciliation and justice to materialise we need forgiveness. Forgiveness opens the door for recognition of guilt, contrition, remorse, confession of guilt that is invited by overwhelming forgiving love, confession of faith which accepts forgiveness, confession of hope which says yes to a new life of sanctification and restitution. South Africans are continually surprised by private and public experiences of this absurd love, this forgiving love. This love is embodied in the life and person of Nelson Mandela. This absurd, forgiving love was experienced at the hearings of the TRC. Manifestations of this love granted South Africa the wonder of a transition to democracy without civil war. The sustainability of our peace is dependent upon our commitment not to make this forgiveness cheap. We live with the hope and expectation that the wonder of a love that forgives will open the gates to a responding love that shows remorse and contrition, that confesses guilt, that repents and repairs, that reconciles and restitutes, that redresses and brings about restorative justice. This absurdity is part of the complexity that we need on the journey away from alienation and injustice like racism, to reconciliation and justice.

7.

We will make good progress to overcome evils like racism and be a truly South African university if we create spaces of constructive proximity on our campuses. In these spaces we nurture public sympathy, public empathy and public interpathy.

American theologian, David Augsberger, provides a helpful definition of sympathy, empathy and interpathy:

> *Sympathy is a spontaneous affective reaction to another's feelings experienced on the basis of perceived similarity between observer and observed. Empathy is an intentional affective response to another's feelings experienced on the basis of perceived differences between the observer and observed. Interpathy is an intentional cognitive and affective envisioning*

of another's thoughts and feelings from another culture, worldview and epistemology (1989: 31).

Reconciliation and justice grow where people do not live outside hearing distance, but where we hear each other, see each other, feel each other, participate and share in each other's lives, in our joys and sorrows, in our guilt and shame, in our anger and pain. An ethos of hybridity might assist us on this journey, i.e. an ethos of intentional creation of spaces of constructive proximity where people mingle, where people develop communal and public sympathy, empathy and interpathy, where boundaries are not rigid but porous so that osmosis can take place, where people get rid of defensive and anxiety-filled minimalist identities, where they develop playful and liberating, cosmopolitan maximalist identities that make us say: yes, I am a Mandelian coloured, but through my hybridic living, my life in proximity and osmosis with my black/white/Indian brothers and sisters I am also more than coloured; yes, I am a Christian, but through my hybridic living with other religious and secular faiths I am more than Christian; yes, I am a South African, but through my osmotic living with brothers and sisters of other African countries I am more than South African; I am African, but through my life in interpathy with people from other continents I am more than African; I am heterosexual but through my hybridic living with people from LGBITQA+ communities I am more than heterosexual; I am male, but through my hybridic living with women I am more than male.

8.

The type of university that enhances life together in diversity is plausible. It is a moral imperative. It opposes discrimination, division and dehumanisation. It is also possible. It draws from the various spiritual, cultural and intellectual resources and traditions of our continent that hunger for and seek life together in diversity, a life of reconciliation and justice. A truly South African university is therefore a university that strives to make a transformative and healing social impact. Through its academic practices like learning and teaching, research and innovation; through its co-curricular practices and professional support services; through its staff, students, alumni and partners; and also through its instruments of sport, arts and culture, such a university impacts in a reciprocal way upon all spheres of society, and this impact is in the direction of togetherness in diversity, reconciliation and justice.

Reference

Augsberger, D. (1989) *Pastoral Counseling Across Cultures*. Westminster: John Knox Press.

Closing Remarks

Achille Mbembe

Look, I cannot highlight enough the importance of platforms such as the one that has brought us together today and I think that we really have to commend Joel and his team for initiating this. I'm also personally grateful to all the speakers, to President Motlanthe who has been, in his usual way, very quiet but extremely intellectually active and to Dr Phosa, who will be speaking in a minute.

Platforms such as this are, as Nico was telling us a moment ago, 'spaces of proximity'. They are absolutely indispensable to the South Africa of today. They are indispensable if we want to detoxify our public sphere. They are also indispensable if we want to deepen democracy in South Africa. And we need to deepen it at a time when globally it is being hollowed out by neo-liberalism, which indeed tends to turn everything into numbers, into what has to be sold and bought; and I would argue that the survival of South Africa as a decent and caring society is inextricably linked to the deepening of democracy. So that's the first thing I wanted to share.

The second is that if indeed we have no choice but to deepen democracy, then the exercise of voice, and of every single voice, becomes a crucial element in the overall project of reopening the future for all. This was a major theme of the discussion this morning. But we have to go further than that. Democracy is not only about the exercise of voice, it is not only about the freedom of expression, it is also about the right to be heard and the right to be listened to and the fact is that we live in a place where historically it has always been extremely difficult for certain categories of people to be listened to or to be heard. This is still the case today. Many people have to scream; they have to shout; they have to burn something; they have to threaten to resort to force before anyone agrees to listen to them. So, the struggle to be heard, it seems to me, is the same as the struggle to be recognised. Only those who are recognised have a chance to be heard and we just have to look around us. Many people are frustrated. They are angry because they have the feeling of not being recognised. They have the feeling of being subjected to permanent misrecognition and, if you want to go forward, we have to bring an end to that.

So how do we foster mutual recognition? It seems to me that this is a very important question that underlay a lot of the discussions we had today. We foster mutual recognition by creating spaces where every day small rituals of mutual recognition are enacted. This is part of how we put in place the pillars of a culture of democracy.

Now this morning we heard a lot about questions of language, narrative, stories and so on and, of course, these are very important questions. Nobody would argue that they are not important. But it is one thing to think of stories, narratives, histories and memories in the exact terms of property and ownership – my story, my narrative, my memory. It is an entirely different proposition to think of this in terms of modes of nationality, that through which I enter into a relationship with another. Most of the time we think of them in the first meaning as property, ownership rather than that through which we enter into a relationship. In order to move ahead, we have to think of them as things I share with others; because, in fact, there is no story or narrative that is only mine. Each human story is by definition, and right from the origins, a story of an encounter with someone else.

So, I have no exclusive property over my story. My story is always by definition already a story involving someone else who, by that very process, becomes co-owner of my story. I think it's important to get back to those fundamentals if only to allow ourselves to ask the right questions about the current moment.

Now a few things about the current moment. I'm sure you all have in mind President Motlanthe's interview with *Business Day*. I heard that he has made peace with COSATU, which is very good. But what is striking in that interview is his attempt to decipher the moment we are in and an attempt to give us elements to chart what the future might be like. What kind of future is it that we can build together and share? It's also a moment that is characterised by the arrival on the political scene of new social protagonists. In fact, what is going on is that a new cultural temperament is emerging, is in the making. We see it in a number of signals, the most important of which is the recent student movement. We see this new cultural temperament in events such as the decolonisation movement, 'Rhodes Must Fall', 'Fees Must Fall', the shift to a vocabulary of almost everything has to fall. For those of you who are addicted to social media there are so many things that are required to fall today. So, what does it mean, the dominance of 'a language of fall' into a language of creation? Why is it that we are so focused on this and that and this, the other person must fall; but nothing on what has to replace it? We talk about destroying that which exists rather than inventing or imagining what it is that we have to put in its place. How we can characterise that deficit of imagination, it seems to me, is a serious political and cultural question.

That having been said, there are questions younger generations are determined to put on the table. For instance, what are the resources of a country for? This is the most fundamental question arising from the FeesMustFall movement. What are they for? What are they for if an important part of these resources cannot be invested in creating a future through education, for instance? And, of course, it is not acceptable from any point of view that only 0.6 per cent to 0.7 per cent of GDP is given to higher education. It's lower than what is given to higher education in neighbouring countries, most of which are poorer than South Africa. It's lower than the amount given by countries of similar levels of development to the same sector. So, what are the resources of a country for? Other questions that are emerging include who is getting what, and why? Who should be getting what, who is entitled to what but is not getting it, and who should be blamed for this? Who owns what and why does it belong to him or her instead of being shared by all? These are questions this generation is asking more and more vehemently.

The other thing is that – listening to some of the presentations this morning – it is as if almost everybody feels hurt. Almost everybody feels treated unfairly. Lots of people are frustrated, they're angry, they are full of rage. So, we have to ask what kind of politics is it that rage, frustration, anger might produce; and how is it that we transcend these primary emotions in order to create something that takes into account the pains of yesterday, the suffering of yesterday, and of today, but puts us on a journey that helps to repair the broken relationships. So, the other thing is that many are no longer willing to wait. There's a 'politics of time' that is shifting. The 'politics of waiting' is being replaced by the 'politics of impatience'. People are willing to sharpen the contradictions; force them into the open and bring them to a point of hopeful resolution and, if necessary, through violence. I cannot tell you the number of young students who have been reading people like Fanon, not only Fanon, but the specific chapter concerning violence. So, violence is once again being considered as a modality of political action. Why?

There's a lot of anger, also, around questions of money, assets, wealth, property and equality; and for valid reasons, because we cannot build a democracy of property in the citizens – it is not sustainable. How do we harness possibilities for people to have a share in the wealth of the nation at a time, first of all, when capital is denationalised and at a time when financials now exceed the sphere of production and manufacture of industrial goods? The last quarter of the twentieth century and the beginning of the twenty-first have seen the rapid development of financial instruments barely imaginable in Karl Marx's times, for instance. So, the question is: what has made this financial explosion possible? Well, it's the idea that risk can be monetised, that we can take risks on risks, which has resulted in a culture of debt. Debt has become the social relation par excellence. Whether one is dealing with questions of housing; even the environment is monetised today through carbon trading and education, through sophisticated methods for creating certain debts.

So, this question of debt, we have to deal with it. We cannot build a democracy of property. Nor can we build a decent society if we do not address the question of indebtedness.

Let me end with two questions. One is on the point of the politics of difference and identity, which is everywhere these days as opposed to the politics of commonality. I think that we thought that, with the end of apartheid, we could transcend the politics of identity and difference, that we could conflate nationalism with what is called 'celebration of difference'. But the celebration of difference cannot be solid ground upon which to build a nation, especially in an era when nationalism is besieged by the forces of capitalist globalisation. And, insofar as capitalist globalisation is about denationalisation and deterritorialisation, we have to find a different way of dealing with the question of identity by highlighting not difference but commonality. We cannot be celebrating our differences: that's what apartheid wanted us to do. What we have to celebrate is what it is that we share and what we share is our common humanity.

Last, we wouldn't do any of this if we kept believing that arts and culture are exactly the same thing as agriculture. In this country we take arts and culture to be the same thing as agriculture. We have a purely instrumentalist understanding of culture, not as a reservoir of imagination, not as a strategic resource for the kind of anticipatory politics that our world is in need of, but as something with which we make money. So there, too, it seems to me, there's a huge need to take the immaterial wealth very seriously if indeed we want to respond to the challenges of our times and if we want South Africa to bring to the world something absolutely original and unique.

Thank you very much.

Mathews Phosa

We are not alone in our thoughts, desires and needs. We are not the same, but we are not different. We are all migrants who arrived in South Africa over centuries, some as recently as yesterday, to call it our home. We must not burden ourselves with the past but empower ourselves with accepting the responsibilities that we share to build a future that is admirable and deserving.

What happened to the excitement of the nation in the lead-up to and the immediate period following the establishment of this fledgling democracy in 1994? Was the aspiration of the father of our nation, Nelson Mandela, not to unite all South Africans under a new flag and a new national anthem?

Everywhere I go I detect an air of anxiety in our everyday lives, some of it economically inspired, some founded in our lack of security and the activities of criminals that have now reached our doorsteps, and others based on an intolerance of each other.

Our leaders, in society and at home, often pitch our reactions to current challenges in our experiences of the past, such as living under apartheid oppression or the remnants of colonialism and other past events.

The time has come to firmly refocus the mind of our nation. We need to regain the excitement of embarking on a new journey that we all felt in 1994. The time for rhetoric and pompous pronouncements belongs in the past if we really want to create a fully inclusive and understanding new order in South Africa.

For this to happen, our leaders must be out there in communities encouraging unity, not only in our distinctive cultural diversity, but also in the multiplicity of the needs and aspirations that unite us all.

As South Africans we must unite to protect our extensive cultural diversity, our past as part of a great trading culture – never forget the people of Mapungubwe – and our unique natural heritage.

Although many efforts are made to protect our natural heritage, it is not only the rhino that needs to be conserved for future generations.

Albert Einstein, in all his scientific glory, once said, 'Our task must be to free ourselves ... by widening our circle of compassion to embrace all living creatures and the whole of nature and its beauty.'

This is not a difficult task in South Africa seeing that we have such a magnitude of inspiring creatures, such as Pickergill's reed frog, the Cape vulture, the cheetah, the yellow-breasted pipits and a multitude of other threatened species that live in our midst.

In gathering at round-tables, conferences, meetings and over dinner at home, we need to deal with matters of importance not only responsibly but also thoroughly.

If we cannot guide and nurture our teenagers with confidence and pride at home, they take their mischievous behaviour with them into the streets of our townships and institutions.

For our democracy to mature past the prolonged teenage years, the leadership of our nation will have to become more proactive and find new solutions to old problems even before they raise their head in public.

Although some may argue that the world is controlled by the nations and the economic powers and currencies of the West, it is also equally influenced by aspects and activities that transpire in the East and those occurring north of our borders on the African continent. If we choose to sit back and wait for somebody to come and rescue our economy or our people, we are living a dream.

Our responsibility as part of a global society is to participate, guide, cultivate and generate new thinking that will ensure local economic and social growth and development.

We must welcome critical debate and thinking that does not

necessarily reflect our own. We must dissect it, discuss it, publicly debate it and form a consolidated opinion that has considered all contributions and aspirations.

Our underperforming economy is a reflection of the impact that the transformation of global society has locally. Our consistent disregard for sound economic growth principles – such as the role of the state versus the role of private enterprise in the creation and protection of employment – is costing our economy and our people dearly.

We can, unfortunately, not continue to dwell in the Kingdom of Mapungubwe. We can be proud of our ancient trading skills and economic strength, but the world of yesterday is not the world of today.

We are living in a new world, one with a population of approximately 7.4 billion people and a net growth of almost seventy million since the beginning of the year. The need to feed them, clothe them, educate them and allow them to become valuable participants in the global economy is extremely challenging and will become even more so in the years to come.

To move forward, we must learn from the lessons of history. It is often convenient to pitch our tents in the past – that way it is easy for us to blame everything that is not working on everyone else – rather than to build our own home of the future with due cognisance of the shortcomings and good things of the past.

The wave of change currently building around the world will catch us off guard if we decide to remain in our past dwellings. By coming together to form responses and make plans to address some of the pressing local and global issues collectively, we will be able to participate in the new order. If not, we run the risk of ending up in the museum; or featuring on the walls in the exhibition halls of the successful.

I don't see a single party in this venue today that is not part of the hope and the future of our country and the African continent. Every one of us has a role to play in making South Africa and Africa great.

We must never forget that this country raised many leaders who positively influenced world events. From the likes of Jan Smuts, Nelson Mandela and other politicians, peace laureates such as

Desmond Tutu, scientists, theologians, artists and many others. South Africa – with only 0,8 percent of the world population – can continue to have an impact internationally.

Every South African, and in the context of this round-table discussion, the Afrikaner, has a role to play in the future of our country. I hear that some of the Afrikaners feel that they are threatened by the government's policies on issues of empowerment, land and quotas in sport.

While this is undeniably true, these are small issues that allow politicians to overlook important matters. Our leaders must be held accountable – we must not allow them to mess with our futures or that of the world.

We need to use platforms such as this to debate and make inputs to government regarding the impact that ill-thought-out or poorly implemented and administered policies are having on our livelihoods and our food security for our nation.

I was once asked by a colleague when someone can be regarded as a South African. Although the question was politically loaded, my response was that South African citizenship can, subject to the provisions of the South African Citizenship Act of 1995, be acquired by birth; descent; naturalisation; and, previously also, by registration in specific instances.

Now what this implies is that, once the above requirements are met, you are a South African and should be respected, protected and valued by the state and other South Africans. Your rights in terms of the Constitution must be respected; and your potential contributions to the economy and society in general should be sought.

Our economy is ambling along at a substandard level as a result of our inability to gather and direct the skills and expertise that are available, as well as from interference by government in employment policies and practices.

Successful nations are built on education, skills development and the harnessing of experience. They also allocate substantial resources to research and development, and to entrepreneurial support.

You noticed no reference to culture, colour or language – only education, skills development and experience!

Let's open the doors and welcome those skilled and experienced Afrikaners and other whites who abandoned their beloved country in search of security and stability; and acknowledge their skills in our economy. Let's make it easy for them to return and to stay.

As for social stability, the momentum of the student challenge of the past weeks appears to be unstoppable and should provide a guide for what may come in the future.

We have seen dissent in the past – protest action, occupation of public spaces, militant rhetoric and destruction of critical infrastructure. We have indeed seen it happen time and again.

Following this, as always, is a nervous middle class joined by business and institutions, scrambling to protect assets and making plans to abandon projects and growth plans.

Often, government is nowhere to be found, arriving on the scene only when the smoke is thick and the security forces are tested to their limits. Then we get the promises, the political jostling for position, and the masses dispersing. They often regroup in another form, with another agenda. But they certainly regroup.

Only time will tell; but be careful, every time it happens it is worse.

Our thoughts, aspirations and wishes for a new South Africa where we all work together for the wellbeing of all is a distant memory. With current events fresh in our memory, we must define the foundations of a new dispensation before further militant action equivalent to that of the 1980s is forced upon us by opportunistic, populist and racist politicians and pseudo leaders.

The exciting road we chose in 1994 is long gone. Deep potholes and divisions are now threatening the very order on which our democracy is built. Populist calls for unfair land alienation and other suicidal economic policies threaten South Africa and its place in Africa and the world. A realisation of the need for change and the establishment of a new economic and social order in South Africa must become a priority.

Although measurable progress was made in a number of areas, prosperity can only become the norm if we abandon the idea that we are a revolutionary state. I call on all our leaders to engage in debate and to ensure that South Africa becomes the society we all desire. South Africa became a constitutional democracy in 1994, and its leaders cannot continue to believe that revolutionary leadership will lead to nation formation and social cohesion.

Careful examination, and planning the extension of tertiary education to include aspects such as the training of health-care professionals, and education colleges and vocational-training institutions, will have to include addressing the critical shortage of skilled and experienced staff at the tertiary education level.

Partnerships and other joint ventures, including calling on qualified professionals in the private sector, need to be sought to alleviate the pressures and shortages experienced in the training and education sector.

Before we seek to become a powerful nation on the continent, we need to grow our economy. With the current debt to GDP level projected to be more than 45 per cent in 2018 (from approximately 28 per cent in 2009) we need to ask serious questions regarding government policies. The current capital expenditure of approximately 12 per cent of the national budget is fast being caught up by the 2015 interest expenditure of 10 per cent of the national budget.

I see trouble on the horizon if we don't address this issue by either cutting the expenditure budget or by emancipation of the economy to provide the required growth in GDP.

The recent and forthcoming increases in taxation are a certain recipe for a further reduction in economic growth in favour of instability and social tension.

We all have a role to play in restoring trust and building mutual respect between all South Africans. Engaging on matters of national importance through round-table debates such as this, and allowing free thinking and engagement in robust debate, form the building blocks of our nation.

In closing: A conflict-free South Africa, reinforced by sustainable economic growth and full employment, will support the long-term economic and political stability of the continent and the world.

Whereas human rights and human development feature equally high with regard to economic stability and development, conflict resolution, the establishment of stable democracies and long-term capital investment and economic growth are preconditions for fairness and regional stability.

A successful and cohesive nation engages in practices where everyone is treated equally, without favour. The law is applied in all aspects of social life consistently and without prejudice. Leaders lead from the front, engaging in constructive debate, taking responsibility for nation-building and condemning corrupt activities.

With powerful, functioning business and community structures such as the Afrikaanse Handelsinstituut, the Afrikaanse Taal en Kultuur Vereniging and local *sakekamers*, the Afrikaners have an important role to play in the development of South Africa.

Our antagonism towards a language, or those speaking it as a first language at home, is often based on our perceptions or lack of information. An analysis of the results of the 2011 census indicated that more black, coloured, and Indian South Africans speak Afrikaans at home than do white South Africans.

According to a study by the South African Institute of Race Relations, only 40 per cent of those who speak Afrikaans at home are white. This means that out of 6.9 million people who speak the language at home, 2.7 million are white, while the rest are from other racial groups.

In short, the results of the 2011 census indicate that Afrikaans is spoken at home by 13.5 per cent of the population, second only to the 22.7 per cent of the population who speak isiZulu at home.

I call on all white Afrikaners to engage in forming an inclusive and cohesive cultural bond between all Afrikaans-speaking South Africans as the foundation for inclusiveness and nation building without elitism and exclusion of other cultural and population groups.

We are all South Africans, be it by birth, descent, naturalisation or other Home Affairs action. Let us not overemphasise whiteness, Afrikaners, Afrikaans or any other popular term. We must all stand up and hold hands to build a future that Madiba can be proud of.

I dare you to do it now – stand up, hold hands – you will realise it is easy and does not require undue effort or energy.

Thank you.

www.ingramcontent.com/pod-product-compliance
Lightning Source LLC
Chambersburg PA
CBHW050537300426
44113CB00012B/2149